THE LINDA GRAY STORY

✪ THE ✪
LINDA
GRAY
STORY

Mark Bego

ST. MARTIN'S PRESS
New York

Design by Debby Jay

Library of Congress Cataloging-in-Publication Data

Bego, Mark.
    The Linda Gray story / by Mark Bego.
        p.   cm.
    ISBN 0–312–01471–6
    1. Gray, Linda, 1940– . 2. Television actors and actresses—United States—Biography. 3. Television producers and directors—United States—Biography. 4. Dallas (Television program) I. Title.
PN1992.4.G73B44 1988
791.45′028′0924—dc19
[B]   87–27325

First Edition

10 9 8 7 6 5 4 3 2 1

To Victoria Green . . .
When I think of "Dallas,"
I think of you.

The author would like to thank the following people for their help and encouragement with this book:

Bart Andrews and Sherry Robb of Andrews & Robb
  Literary Agents
Richard Baker
Mark Chase
Audrey Kaufmann
Mark Lasswell
Toni Lopopolo of St. Martin's Press
David Salidor
Caroline O'Connell
Marie Morreale
and, of course, Sam and Martha!

Contents

★ 1 ★

Meet Linda Gray

To television audiences around the world, she is known as the ultra-chic but emotionally brittle Sue Ellen Ewing, the long-suffering, masochistic wife of the dastardly J.R. on the long-running hit series "Dallas."

Linda Gray in real life is one of Hollywood's most popular Renaissance women. She is a self-sufficient, open-minded, outspoken, determined, talented, and super-confident single woman. To her millions of international fans, Linda is a prime example that a glamorous life can indeed begin after forty.

While most actresses would be content to glide effortlessly through their tenth season in a hit TV series, Linda constantly seeks new challenges. Having already appeared in several films, she has her sights set on Broadway, additional films, and beyond. Obsessed with learning and experiencing everything that she can about all aspects of show business, she is the only female cast member of "Dallas" to have directed episodes of the show. She insists that this is only the beginning of her career and that acting is only one part of the total package.

"I'm living proof that age is not a barrier to success," she proclaims glowingly. "Age is meaningless. I keep getting younger. Some people are old at thirty, while others remain young forever. Age stems from all the stuff you carry in your head—the negative stuff— that should be dumped daily, like garbage."

Not only does she preach openness and self-actualization, but she lives her own philosophy as well. In 1973, at the age of thirty-two, she was a happily married woman raising two preteen children. Wed at the age of twenty-one, Linda had already been a successful model who had dabbled in acting and made over 400 television commercials, plus roles as an extra in several feature films. Suddenly, to the astonishment of her successful art director husband, Ed Thrasher, she announced that not only was she going to study acting, but that she would seek to resume the acting career that she had once left behind her.

"I was a housewife and mother, washing diapers," she recalls. "I said to myself, 'Is this all there is to life?' The next day I hired a housekeeper, defied my family training, and began to study for a career as an actress. At age thirty-two, it took guts to begin acting classes. Suddenly, I was a student, studying acting with eighteen-year-olds. But as strange as I felt, I felt good. It was what I wanted to do."

With the wholehearted encouragement of her drama coach, Linda soon landed guest-starring roles on television shows such as "McCloud," "Switch," and "Marcus Welby, M.D." Her first big break in television came in the short-lived and controversial Norman Lear-produced series, "All That Glitters," in which she portrayed a transsexual named Linda Murkland.

When that show ended, in late 1977 she auditioned for an upcoming TV mini-series about the power struggles of a wealthy Texas family. Little did she realize at the time that this chapter in her blossoming career was destined to change her entire life.

The name of the mini-series was "Dallas," and no one then involved in the project could have guessed at the impact it would ultimately have. "Sue Ellen didn't even have a name!" Linda laughingly recalls of the initial five-episode series when it was filmed in 1978. "It was just a four-line part. In order for me to read for the part, they had to create dialogue just for the audition. Sue Ellen was just a visual. She wasn't even identified as J.R.'s wife. They just wanted someone to sit on the couch and look like an ex-Miss Texas. I arrived; I was tall and brunette. I looked the part. I think I got it more on my looks than anything."

The original mini-series was shot on location, over a two-month period, under the hot Texas sun. This gave Linda her first taste of independence away from her family. When the series was given the go-ahead as a regular weekly program, it was an opportunity that she wouldn't have dreamed of refusing. However, she recalls that her husband was less than thrilled by her new-found success away from home.

Although a successful acting career was exactly what she had been courting all along, when faced with sudden fame, Linda admits that it was a bit overwhelming. According to her, "I had to learn to be a star. There should be courses in how to handle success. Because it's not easy, wonderful as success is. Often it seems that when you least expect it, a giant wind comes and whisks you away—if you let it. But you hang on to your bedpost for dear life. At least I did."

Suddenly she found herself in the middle of a flurry of activity. As an actress, Linda quickly proved to be so captivating a counterpart to her "Dallas" co-star Larry Hagman's portrayal of the evil J.R. that it wasn't long before Sue Ellen became one of the show's pivotal characters.

In the beginning, Sue Ellen had so few lines of dialogue that Linda had to look for ways to make the most of her time on camera. She said, recalling her strategy, "Dammit, if they weren't going to write any words for me, I'd give them something through my eyes. I did research into Southern ladies. I found out that they could kill you with a look—smile and chop your head off in the same breath. So I set about creating Sue Ellen."

For Linda, one of the most enjoyable aspects of playing Sue Ellen was the opportunity to play a woman on television who was completely different from herself. Unlike Sue Ellen, who lived in the shadow of her tyrannical husband and turned to the liquor bottle and scandalous affairs to solve her problems, Linda found herself becoming stronger and more self-determined all the time. When the hectic pace of being a working mother began to get her down, Gray took positive action and found a therapist.

Dealing with the repression of her strict Catholic upbringing and problems with her husband, who was not happy with her new occupation, Linda recalls, "I had to search for myself, to look deep inside for answers. I was so confused, so upset, that I went into therapy and stayed in it for more than three years. I finally learned how to say 'Yes' to me, and 'No' to others. I had always let other people tell me what to do. I was like a marionette with lots of people pulling the strings. I had no personality. I was a chameleon."

Linda was moving and growing as a person. By this point her two children, Jeff and Kehly, were teenagers who were becoming more independent; now it was Mom's turn to step out of her shell as well. "I look back and see how far I've come and all I've overcome," she says. "Years ago, when people would ask me how I felt, I didn't know. I was always playing the good little girl. My childhood and my schooling and the church were so restrictive and repressive. I took everyone's rules for my own and put them on my head. And they weighed so damn much. My whole thing was to please everyone else. I was raised to believe nice girls don't do this, and they certainly don't do *that*. Acting was just one of the things nice girls don't do. I didn't shake any of those taboos for years. I had to learn."

As Linda Gray grew, so did the character of Sue Ellen Ewing. Linda wasn't always happy with the things that the show's writers were having Sue Ellen do. Linda felt that the character was stagnating, becoming too stereotyped as an unhappy, drunken lush. At one point in her "Dallas" career, several newspapers intimated that Linda too had a drinking problem. "I guess it's a compliment," shrugs Linda in retrospect. "You do your job so well people assume that's who you are. There never has been and never will be a problem. I get giggly on half a glass of champagne.

I've lived an ordered life and been into health foods for twenty-five years."

During her annual time off from the mid-June to March shooting schedule of "Dallas," instead of relaxing and resuming her former role as a housewife, Linda took advantage of her schedule to take on new assignments. She sought out and landed further acting roles on several made-for-TV movies, where she could stretch out as an actress. She played a jealous turn-of-the-century belle in "The Two Worlds of Jenny Logan"; Leland Hayward's second wife in "Haywire"; and a divorcée making a new life for herself in "Not in Front of the Children." She also hosted an educational program about sexuality called "The Body Human," and made several guest appearances on variety shows. Instead of being content to rest on her laurels, Linda instead looked for fresh challenges.

Fitness had always been important to her, and when she turned forty in 1980, she showed the world just how sexy a woman of that age could be. It wasn't long before Linda began appearing more and more frequently on the covers of major U.S. and international magazines. She has gone on to become a shining example of how a woman of the eighties can continue to look better and better with the passage of time.

While Linda's career was thriving, her marriage, unfortunately, was not. By 1983 she had found that, after twenty-one years of marriage, she and her husband had reached an impasse. When the marriage ended, their split-up became one of the most publicized divorces of the decade.

Although Ed Thrasher has his own lucrative career as a Grammy Award-winning graphic artist, (for designing album covers), he had steadily grown resentful of Linda's new—and highly visible—life-style. Since her children were at a more independent age, Linda realized that it was time to make a move toward her own independence.

"Ed's very negative, and I chose to be positive," Linda explains of her ultimate decision to leave Thrasher. "It was a simple question of survival. I had to get out. I knew if I stayed he would never leave. So I rented a house in Malibu, but because of my reclusiveness and my need for privacy, I said nothing to the press. Well, it leaked out anyhow that I had rented a beach house, that my kids were there, and that it wasn't summer. The tabloids became enamored of what was happening, and they invented everything from there on out."

Since Linda's rented Malibu house was in such close proximity to Larry Hagman's, it was theorized that Gray and Hagman were having an affair. The truth was that Larry and his wife Maj were Linda's most supportive friends during the ordeal of her divorce.

"We're still friendly, and he'll always be Daddy to my children," Linda says of Ed. "But I choose not to see him. Relationships have time limits. When you've both given as much as you can, the need arises to release each other to find happiness elsewhere."

Sometimes life does imitate art. It was in the autumn of 1983 that Sue Ellen began to have an affair on the show with a much younger man, played by actor Christopher Atkins. Meanwhile, in real life, Linda Gray began a three-year romance with a trumpet player named Paul Constanza. Paul was ten years younger than Linda, and the gossip merchants had a field day when the news leaked out.

Since her subsequent break-up with Constanza, Linda's beaux have always been younger than she. It is probably due to the fact that she thinks of herself as being younger than her chronological age. "In my mind, I am about twenty-seven," she proclaims. "I don't think about age when I date. Younger men are supportive. They're encouraging and they're fascinated by older women."

Linda Gray's life just gets more and more fascinating. When her contract was due to lapse on "Dallas" in 1985, Linda knew that her position on the show was so solid that she demanded she be allowed to direct at least one show per season, just as her male co-stars Larry Hagman, Patrick Duffy, and Steve Kanaly do from time to time. According to her, "Nothing in life is accidental. Things happen when you're really ready. When you're 'together,' willing to risk something new." She ended up getting her way and has directed one episode in each of her subsequent seasons on "Dallas." This matter reportedly infuriated fellow cast member Victoria Principal, who did not have as much clout on the show as Linda obviously does.

At one point in her "Dallas" career Linda Gray complained that Sue Ellen was becoming stagnant as a drunken victim of life, but the writers on the show have since allowed the character to grow and develop. Now Linda proclaims, "I love Sue Ellen." She admits that there are more and more similarities between actress and character as time goes by. During the 1986–1987 season on "Dallas," audiences delighted in seeing Sue Ellen really blossom and come into her own—just as Linda has in reality.

"I think Sue Ellen is the most fascinating woman on TV today," says Gray. "She's constantly changing. She has been a bitch, she's been an adulteress. A lot of people can relate to Sue Ellen. What we do on 'Dallas' is to really exaggerate those human problems. She's gone through more changes—and come through more problems—than any other character on television. She's a survivor—and so am I." Although Linda Gray has never been a bitch, an adulteress, or a drunk, she has grown and has emerged stronger as she has solved her own personal problems. That is probably why Linda is so believable as the character of Sue Ellen.

"Becoming a star late in life is not a minus but a plus," Gray insists. "I have something extra to bring to my work and to people. The something extra is 'Me.' I have absolutely no regrets about not having made it sooner. I certainly don't miss not having lived in the fast lane because that's not me. Also, I'm a firm believer that life happens when it means to. Many times, between the years of struggle and Sue Ellen, I thought about quitting, but a little voice inside said to press on. Yes, it was frustrating, even hurtful, being in the starting gate for such a long time waiting for someone to fire the gun. But when someone finally did, I took off like a rocket because I was ready."

Do those sound like the words of a shy girl from Culver City, California, who went to school across the street from MGM Studios, too frightened to admit that she wanted to become an actress when she grew up? Does this sound like someone who once almost married a man that her parents told her she would learn to love in time? Does this sound like someone who was once a proper little housewife and mother from the Los Angeles suburbs whose only concern was what to serve for dinner? She's obviously come a long way.

The Linda Gray Story

Linda Gray's story is one of goals, challenges, growth, and self-determination. She's taken control of her own life, and molded herself into a creative, content, and confident individual. At one point in her life she was afraid to speak up and voice her own opinions, but now she has become a role model for other women who want to take control of their lives.

What drove Linda Gray to pursue her dreams when she was already settled as a wife and mother? What made her become stronger and more determined to realize her own goals? What is it like to be an international star on "Dallas"? What is the truth about her much-publicized feud with Victoria Principal? Where does Sue Ellen Ewing end, and Linda Gray begin? How does she stay fit, and what are her secrets about how to look fabulous after forty?

The answers to these questions are part of the total Linda Gray story. Hers is not only a story of the quest for personal fulfillment, but a saga of survival. There is only one person who calls the shots in her life—and that is Linda Gray herself!

★ 2 ★

Linda's Childhood

Culver City, California, will always have a significant spot in show-business history as the location of MGM Studios, where so many memorable film classics have been produced. In 1938, when *Gone with the Wind* was being filmed at MGM, the studio was confident that it was creating a movie classic, so all of the details had to be perfect. Among the props needed for the film was an aristocratic-looking fob for the pocket watch carried by Rhett Butler (Clark Gable). Someone at the studio knew of a local watchmaker who could craft such a piece of jewelry: the man's name was Les Gray.

Little did Les suspect at the time, when he created Clark Gable's *Gone with the Wind* watchfob, that it was not to be his only contribution to show business. Ironically, it was at those same studios that the interiors to a show called "Dallas" would be videotaped, with his yet-unthought-of daughter as part of the cast. It seems like a strange twist of fate, but that was exactly what came to happen!

It was on September 12, 1940, that Les's wife Marge gave birth to the first of their two daughters. The baby girl was delivered by Dr. Richard T. Beem, and the Grays decided to name her Linda. Years later the doctor's wife, Dorothy Beem was to recall, "She was the prettiest baby my husband ever delivered—and he delivered 3,500 during his career!"

During Linda's first five years, however, there were several close calls that could have tragically marred or ended her life. When she was two years old, Linda was out for a walk with her mother when she suddenly bolted into a busy street full of traffic and barely missed being struck by a moving car.

Marge Gray distinctly remembers the episode. "She darted out into the busy street between two parked cars," she explains. "My heart stopped as she disappeared, and all I heard was the shrill squeal of brakes. I said, 'Oh, God, no!' and ran out into the road expecting to find my baby lying dead beneath the wheels of a car. Instead, there was Linda, standing very wobbly about two inches from the car's bumper. The poor driver almost had a heart attack. If he hadn't reacted quickly, she'd have been dead for sure."

When Linda was four, she went on a vacation with her parents in Palm Springs. One morning during their visit, Linda was left unattended for a few minutes in the vicinity of the swimming pool in their hosts' backyard. "I was helping make the beds when we heard a splash from the pool," says Marge. "We dashed to the window, and all we could see were two little hands disappearing below the water. We raced to the pool, and my friend dived in and pulled my daughter from the deep end. Linda was unconscious and turning blue. I laid her down on the deck and started mouth-to-mouth resuscitation. The seconds seemed like hours as her little body lay as still as death beneath me. Then suddenly she started to cough and opened her eyes. I clutched her to me and thanked God."

It was only months after the swimming pool incident that little Linda began complaining of dizzy spells. According to her mother, "She couldn't walk without collapsing. I took her to the doctor, who said she had polio and that her chances of survival were poor. We refused to send her to the hospital because we were told we could give her better attention at home by using the Kenny Method. This was a revolutionary method of treating polio victims by using massage and hot water. My husband Leslie and I took turns sitting up with her around the clock. And gradually we got those weak limbs to respond. It wasn't long before she was back to her old self again."

Linda was always a pretty, well-dressed, and proper little girl. Her parents are devout Catholics, and every Sunday, Linda and her sister Betty would attend church with them, attired in their best little dresses and shoes. Childhood friend Cathy Dietrichs still recalls, "Everyone would turn to look at Linda because she looked so lovely."

Remembering what it was like when she began to attend school, Linda explains, "I'm from a strict Catholic background, so naturally I went to St. Augustine School and Notre Dame Academy." She especially remembers attending classes every day in her "little Catholic schoolgirl's uniform."

It was while in grammar school that the lure of

show business beckoned Linda from behind the MGM Studio gates. "St. Augustine was just across the street from MGM," says Linda. "I was a curb-sitter between classes, waiting for stars like Judy Garland, Spencer Tracy, and Mickey Rooney to come out so I could ask for autographs. Mr. Tracy was my special hero. I met him later, and he said, 'Kid, when you don't have lines to say, use your eyes. They can do all the work to connect you with your audience.'"

Other MGM stars whom Linda collected autographs from at the front gates included Elizabeth Taylor and Ann Miller. Years later, when she was appearing on the 1982 television special, "Night of 100 Stars," which was taped at Radio City Music Hall, Linda ran into Mickey Rooney and Ann Miller for the first time since her childhood as a star-struck autograph seeker. She was running over to Ann and Mickey to remind them of the event, but stopped dead in her tracks. She laughingly recalled reconsidering her well-intended remembrance: "I thought, when you come up to someone and you say, 'I remember you when I was a kid' . . . well, they might not be thrilled about that!" She ultimately chose not to recount her story to the veteran stars.

It was from hanging out in front of MGM that Linda first began to fantasize about becoming an actress when she grew up. When she announced her career goal to her mom and dad, however, her dreams were met with strong disapproval. "Nobody in my family was too excited about it. My parents were very strict, and to them, acting was one step above being a hooker," says Gray.

Weekend movie matinees fueled Linda's love for the world of make-believe up on the silver screen.

"I would run down to the Culver Theatre every Saturday afternoon to see Howard Keel sing to Kathryn Grayson in MGM's *Showboat,* or to watch Stewart Granger and Deborah Kerr. I was in love with Stewart Granger in *King Solomon's Mines,"* she recalls. She couldn't have imagined then that years later she would co-star with Howard Keel on "Dallas!"

As she grew older, her dreams seemed to slip farther and farther from her grasp, as she found herself turning into an awkward adolescent. "It was hard for me, considering I was the ugliest kid you could ever imagine. I was five feet seven inches in sixth grade, which is gigantic. I had a beanpole figure consisting of long black stringy hair, big eyes, and buckteeth which made it difficult for me to close my mouth. Soon I had braces on my teeth and a face full of acne. I was a terribly unattractive kid. I didn't even date very much when I first went to high school because I was really an ugly duckling. Because of my awful looks, the kids would taunt me. They called me 'bean pole' and 'bug eyes' and other names as well. Sometimes I'd get so upset I'd cry." In her quest to find some meaning in her life, at one point during her high-school years, Linda almost found herself being talked into becoming a nun!

Naturally, as time went on, the ugly duckling grew into a beautiful swan. "My parents became worried because I was so shy. I was always sweating and afraid to look men in the eyes. Somehow my body formed into the frame of a young woman instead of the incredible two-headed transplant. Suddenly everything just began to fall into place. The boys got taller. Braces straightened my teeth . . . and I became homecoming queen during my senior year."

However, to make the transition complete, Linda's parents enrolled her in a Dale Carnegie class just as she was entering high school, to help her overcome her shyness. The course was being taught by a neighbor named Cliff Bollman. Linda was so shy that her aunt, Ruth Gray Hartinian, attended the class with her to make sure that she got through it.

Cliff Bollman especially remembers Linda's terminal shyness. "In the first few sessions, she couldn't speak at all. She couldn't even get her name out. She was that nervous." But he points out that it wasn't long before "she just blossomed like a rose." Her Aunt Ruth was later to comment, "She really had a bubbly personality afterwards. She was like a new person."

After taking the course, Linda found that she had enough confidence to try out for theatrical productions in school. As she explains it, "Despite my shyness, it was easy for me to get up in front of people on the stage. I don't know how. I just did it and enjoyed it, and everyone was surprised."

It was during her junior year at the all-girl Notre Dame Academy that she made her theatrical debut. As she recalls, "We decided that for a spring play we would do *Sleeping Beauty*. We said, 'Well, we need a Prince Charming.' I looked the other way—but everyone said, 'Linda, what about you?' I thought, 'I have a pageboy [haircut], and I'm perfect for the part'—so I agreed. They put me in tights and white satin bloomers like Prince Charming would wear, and I had a hat with a plume. I was a wonderful Prince Charming. The night we did the play, I was sailing through it. Toward the end, right before I kissed Sleeping Beauty to make her wake up, I walked down in front of the curtain to deliver a monologue. A little girl sitting in the front row next to her mother looked at me and blurted out, 'Mommy, Prince Charming has boobs!'

"At that point I totally lost the character. I just stared and thought, 'My acting career is over before it's even begun.' I even got hysterical for a few seconds. Then I thought, 'I can't let it get the better of me.' So I walked over to Sleeping Beauty, threw my hat down, bent over, and kissed her to wake her up. There was a big finale, but I was still devastated. I thought, 'My big moment and I'm ruined by a kid!' It was then I realized how audiences can have a great effect on an actor's performance. Maybe that's why I want to end up on Broadway—I just won't play Prince Charming!"

Linda's next theatrical experience came from a play that the all-girl Notre Dame Academy did in conjunction with an all-boy school. "We joined forces and did a production of *Our Town*. I won some sort of an award playing Emily. I always wanted to do this [acting] desperately, so I broached the subject with my parents. Of course it was totally unacceptable because they wanted me to be a nurse, or an airline stewardess, or a teacher, or a civil-servant kind of person."

Of course, since she was attending an all-girl school there would be occasional slumber parties where the students would stay up all night talking about the nuns and boys. As happens with most teenagers, the temptation to try liquor when the parents aren't around got the better of Linda and her friends at one of their all-night parties. Linda remembers, "I think the first and only time I ever got drunk was at a slumber party in my senior year at high school when we threw different kinds of alcohol into a pitcher and

drank it all. We wound up on the floor throwing up—
it was just awful!"

After graduating from high school, Linda decided to
continue her education at a coed college in Santa
Monica. The very first day she noticed that there was a
big difference between that and attending an all-girl
Catholic school. When she walked into her French
class and noticed her professor staring at her shapely
legs, she knew she was going to have fun in this more
liberal atmosphere. "I remember smiling to myself and
thinking, 'Aha, this is a little different than the glare of
nuns bearing sturdy rulers!' At that point, men became an important part of my life."

While still a teenager, Linda was almost pushed into
a marriage that she didn't want. She nearly flipped
when she found out that her parents were conspiring
with the interested beau to rush her to the altar. "I'll
never forget it," says Linda. "I was dating this land-
scape architect. He was terrific. Adorable. I loved
going out with him and we were great buddies . . . I
thought. One night we were driving home and he
stopped at a stop sign. He reached in his pocket, took
out a little box, and handed me an engagement ring.

"I was shocked. I gasped, 'What's this?' I came
home hysterical and crying, and Mom and Dad woke
up and wanted to know what was the matter. 'Dick
gave me this ring,' I cried. 'Yes, I know. He bought it
at my store,' Dad said. 'But, Daddy, why didn't you
tell me?' I yelled. By now my mom was out of bed
making tea, and they were both trying to comfort me.
'Honey, it's all right,' they said, like a Greek chorus.
'You'll learn to love him.' I couldn't believe it! 'Learn
to love him!?' What kind of love was that?

"For the first time in my life, I rebelled. I gave Dick

back his ring and explained I wasn't ready for marriage. I hadn't really grown up. It was a big step for me—the first decision I'd ever really made on my own."

This episode made Linda realize that no matter what, she would have to take responsibility for her own life. Up to this point she had basically allowed herself to go along with the decisions that her parents and teachers made for her. Although she developed a certain sense of independence from her psychology classes at Santa Monica College, and later at UCLA, she realized that she wasn't in full control of her life. It was suddenly clear to her that other people were making choices about her destiny.

Linda finally saw that it was up to her to make her own dreams come true. She secretly longed to get involved in show business, and she was suddenly aware that her fate was truly in her own hands. Before long she had dropped out of college and started her modeling career.

★ 3 ★

Modeling, Marriage, and Motherhood

It was really a strange turn of events that led young Linda Gray to a lucrative modeling career. When she was still eighteen years old, she and her mother attended a fashion show at her school. While she expected to pick up a few fashion tips for the upcoming season, she had no idea that she was about to embark on a brand-new career.

As she recalls, "My mother and I were sitting at the bottom of the runway watching the models, and there was a photographer there snapping pictures. The following week he came to the school and demanded to know who that was in the picture. They asked, 'The model?' 'No,' he said, 'the girl in the back of all my pictures.' They replied, 'Oh, that's one of our students.' He wanted to meet me. So, accompanied by my mother, I went to meet him. He said, 'I'd like to take some pictures of you.'" Together, Linda and her cameraman came up with a suitable resume shot, and the photographer began to send her out on casting calls for television commercials. According to Linda, she'll never forget her first resume photo: "That one shot launched me on a modeling career!"

Naturally, Les and Marge Gray were still appalled at their teenage daughter's claims that she intended to become an actress instead of a psychologist. The idea of modeling seemed like a happy medium. As Linda explains it, "My parents were still opposed to my becoming an actress, but we compromised with modeling, and I began to learn the lighting and technical aspects of the productions while I was doing commercials."

According to Linda, "It was at a time when stars didn't do commercials because it was beneath their dignity. They told me I had the all-American look— big eyes, long hair, a big smile—they said I'd be great for Pepsi commercials. 'Terrific,' I said, and I started working. At nineteen, I was making $28,000 a year. So, I thought, 'School is boring; I'm bored with biology, anthropology; I want out of here.' I left. That's how it started, but all the time I knew I was going to end up where I am today—or further. I always knew."

Linda seemed a natural at modeling, and it wasn't long before she had an agency to represent her. One television commercial led to another; she did print modeling for magazines and newspapers as well. She was thrilled to find that she could make so much money at something that was so much fun.

Did Linda ever regret dropping out of college to become a model? Not really. According to her, "The commercials started to happen. I started making a ton of money and thought, 'That's more exciting than anthropology!'"

Her modeling career also led to an increasing interest in nutrition. "When I started modeling," says Linda, "I also started trying all the diets; I went through every phase. But I'd lose five pounds and gain them back immediately. I realized the silliness of it all and began to rely on good nutrition, something I learned . . . before it was a fad. Actually, my mother raised us on simple foods—partly because she hated to cook—so I learned to love vegetables, wheat germ, bran."

It was through one of the modeling assignments her agency sent her out on that she met the man she would eventually marry. There was an audition call for an attractive model to appear on the cover of an album that Capitol Records was planning to release. The art director who designed the album cover was Ed Thrasher.

According to Linda, "My agency described me in such glowing terms that when Ed was looking for a model he said to them, 'If she's that great, I'll marry her!'"

She wasn't quite sure what to expect when she arrived at Capitol Records. "I got to his office," she continues, "and he asked me to lift my skirt. He needed someone with great legs. I lifted my skirt to about mid-knee. He said, 'Is that it?' I said that was it. He hired me anyway."

While Linda stood there in Ed's office, he telephoned her modeling agent. When Thrasher got the agent on the phone he said, "Sitting in front of me is a tall brunette with enormous eyes, a beautiful smile, and the greatest pair of legs you've ever seen." Recalls Linda, "It was nauseating. I was so embarrassed!"

Linda posed for the album cover photos, and Ed began asking her out on dates. This was in 1959, when Linda was still eighteen years old.

At first Linda wasn't interested in Ed's advances. But eventually he wore down her resistance. Says Linda, "Ed kept asking me out to dinner, and for months I kept turning him down. I thought he was just another Hollywood playboy. Besides being so terribly naive, I had never dated anyone in show business. But he was persistent. He bombarded me with clever cards and sketches—he was also a cartoonist— and pleadings for dates. Finally, I couldn't ignore him any longer. I had to take him seriously."

She went out with him, and found him to be quite sweet and sincere. She continued to date Ed over the next three years, and continued her modeling career. She began appearing in many different television commercials, playing housewives and glamour girls, for clients from Alberto VO-5 shampoo to United Airlines.

Her career in commercials progressed at a steady pace, and so did her relationship with Ed. In 1962 Linda and Ed were married. Up to that point, Linda laughs, "There was a lot of heavy breathing going on, but I swear I was the only twenty-one-year-old virgin married that year. My mother and my church told me that was the way it was supposed to be, and I bought it."

Based on her contacts in the commercial business,

Linda landed featured roles in two motion pictures in 1963: *Under The Yum Yum Tree,* starring Jack Lemmon and Carol Lynley; and *Palm Springs Weekend,* which starred Troy Donahue and Connie Stevens.

A year later Linda gave birth to a son, Jeff. Two years later, her daughter Kehly was born. The remainder of the 1960s were Linda Gray's heavy-duty housewife and mother years. Once the kids had started school, Linda found more time to do TV commercials. It was easy to get to work as Linda and Ed still lived in the Los Angeles area. Ed was happy with it, as long as it didn't interfere with her household duties. "He did like me doing commercials, because I brought in a lot of money," explains Linda.

By 1970 Ed had developed a yen to move out of Los Angeles and live in the country. He located a piece of property that he was keen on buying in the Canyon Country, an hour's drive north of Hollywood. Linda recalls her feelings about the move: "I'm a city girl," she complained, "and I thought, 'I don't want to live out here, it's a mess.' He finally convinced me."

The three-acre lot that they ended up buying was thickly wooded; in fact, the property had thirty-five statuesque oak trees, and plenty of room for them to raise horses and plant gardens. "Because it was in the earthquake area," recalls Linda, "we wanted a one-story home. It was supposed to be finished in January 1971, but it wasn't, so we lived in a trailer for six months, moving into the house as soon as workmen found us space. Even though we had to wrap everything, including ourselves, in drop cloths or plastic, we loved our house." Late in 1971 the construction was completed, and Linda set about furnishing and decorating the house in a very comfortable and informal

Early American mode, with hand-woven Indian rugs and many western ranch touches.

The fifteen room ranch-type house had a big kitchen with a large butcher-block table and plenty of space for Linda to assemble her favorite recipes. "I told the architect I wanted to live in a kind of tree house," she remembers. Since the house was surrounded by trees and thick foliage, Linda chose to have several large, floor-to-ceiling windows, and no drapes. The house had a nice, woodsy, open feeling, the perfect setting for her to play housewife and full-time mommy.

However, even though the house had a swimming pool, a tennis court, cats, dogs, and eventually horses, Linda didn't feel at all content with the happy housewife routine. She longed for something more.

After comparing notes with a girlfriend one day, Linda decided that the thrill had gone out of being a model. "My girlfriend was always coming to me with these great stories about photographers and other men propositioning her," says Linda. "I wondered what was wrong with me. Why didn't I get propositioned? All the time as a model, I thought the lack of action meant I was terribly unattractive. It finally dawned on me that it was because of the image I projected. I'd come into a room and say 'Hi, I'm Linda Gray.' But the sub-context was, 'I'm married, have two point two children, three dogs, two cats, two horses—and stay away!'" She was bored with being a housewife who dabbled in modeling. She had always wanted to be an actress. How long was she going to wait? By now she was thirty-two, and she thought it was about time she started doing what she really wanted to do with her life.

Linda explains, "I started out doing commercials. I

thought, 'Isn't this wonderful? All I have to do to make a lot of money is smile.' But I needed more stimulation, more creative challenge. So I decided to enroll in an acting class."

Not surprisingly, Ed hated the idea, and couldn't fathom Linda's rationale for it. "I was determined," Linda remembers. "But he was scared. He said, 'What is this? Why do you want to be an actress? Don't you have enough?' I told him I loved him and the children too much to think of throwing it all away to be an actress, and I told him, 'We'll find a way to work it out.'

"But Ed said, 'Why don't you wait until the kids are in college?' I sat down and thought to myself, 'My God! I'll be a character actress if I wait till then!' It suddenly hit me that it was okay for me to do what was good for my family, but when I started rocking the boat, saying what *I* wanted, it made everyone uncomfortable." In the end, Linda realized that she had to do what she wanted to do, or she would never feel fulfilled as an individual. With that in mind, she went ahead and enrolled in the acting class.

This was, without a doubt, the most daring thing that she had attempted in all of her married years. The last exciting challenge that she had embarked upon was in 1965 when she tried out for the "Miss Rheingold" beauty contest, sponsored by the Rheingold Brewing Company. She ended up placing sixth in that competition. To Linda, enrolling in the class now was a contest to see if she could accomplish what she wanted to in life, and she was determined to finish in first place this time around!

"At thirty-two, it took guts to begin acting classes," Linda admits. "All my women friends had married, retired from work, and were raising babies. I thought: 'Doing commercials, home, family . . . who'd want more?' But there was always a creativity inside me, yearning to burst forth. Ed never knew what I really wanted. Once I took the stand that 'this is what I want,' it scared Ed. I resented that, though I understood. It was fear of the unknown."

With that, Linda plunged right in. She left the "PTA meetings, homemade butter, [and] car pools" behind her, and off to acting class she went. "I took classes with drama coach Charles Conrad along with Veronica Hamel, Carl Weathers, Susan Blakely, and others—all of them much younger than I was," says Gray.

She excelled in the courses. According to her, "By the time my drama teacher felt I was ready, my family was reasonably prepared and quite comfortable with the thought of me being an actress."

Oddly enough, Linda's first big acting opportunity came from a chance meeting. "Just because I got friendly in a health-food store with a woman who turned out to be Mrs. Dennis Weaver, I got a small part in Dennis' 'McCloud' series, which led to other small parts in other Universal shows," she recalls.

Linda feels that her drama coach, Charles Conrad, really made all the difference in the world when it came to building up her confidence. "He was more than my coach," she says. "He was my guru and my shrink. He was very pivotal in my life. It's amazing how people come into your lives when you need them. He really made me take a look at what was inside me so that I could bring it out."

It wasn't long before her acting teacher had so much confidence in her that he tossed her out of the nest. She was ready to try her wings. "Charles Conrad, my drama coach, eventually kicked me out, sent me into the big world, and I went to read for a guest shot on 'Marcus Welby, M.D.' I got it—a 6 A.M. Monday call!"

On Linda's debut appearance on "Marcus Welby, M.D.," a case of nerves almost got the best of her. According to Linda, "Over the weekend I developed a psychosomatic toothache, and they had to roll my hair over and shade like hell to cover this gigantic abscessed jaw!"

While on the Universal set, Linda's work on episodes of "McCloud" and "Marcus Welby, M.D." was so appreciated that she ended up appearing on "Big Hawaii," "Emergency!" and "Switch" as well. These shows provided a good training ground for Linda's career in front of the camera.

She remembers a particular episode of "Marcus Welby, M.D." that taught her a valuable lesson about hair, make-up, and one's confidence level. "I had only four lines, and I hated the hair and make-up. But I thought the professional thing to do was to go on, so I did. Afterward, I happened to be talking with a prominent agent, and he advised me, 'Never go in front of a camera unless you feel you look terrific. If you don't look your best, nobody watching that program is going to think of blaming the hairdresser or make-up artist.' And I think he was right. So now I know that if I'm uncomfortable, I can't concentrate as well." (In later years this lesson caused Linda to change Sue Ellen's hair on "Dallas," in spite of what the show's producers thought. "I realized Sue Ellen's look had to be looser," she explains. "I had to get away from that helmet-head of hair.")

Linda soon found that while she was becoming more content as an actress, the strain on her personal life was beginning to take its toll. It was at this point that she began therapy in hopes of solving the internal tug-of-war between her acting career and her home life with Ed.

"I felt unfulfilled," remembers Linda," and I knew something had to be done. I went into therapy, and later my husband joined me. Happily, we were able to reach an understanding. It was my idea to go for therapy. But my husband was reluctant. He wasn't hostile about therapy—he just thought it was for people who had problems, and he didn't think that he had any problems. I finally convinced him that it wasn't my problem or his problem. He realized that we were married and it was *our* problem. And it was much better when he joined the group. Once we sorted things out, he realized that I wasn't going to run away to Rome and elope with Marcello Mastroianni. He saw that I wasn't going to leave him and the children, but that I had to do what I had to do—no matter what.

"Going to therapy was the most positive thing I've done in my whole life. An awful lot of love evolved from it all. What it did was strengthen the beautiful marriage and family life we already had. Therapy helped me unlike anything else ever has. It's shocking to realize that we know more about our microwave ovens than we do about what's happening in our own heads. But I've always been incredibly curious about what's going on inside of me—and the exploration of it all opened me up, freed me, made me realize how valuable I was as a human being."

In the mid-1970s Linda and Ed's careers were both on the move. Thrasher and co-artist Christopher

Whorf won a Grammy for their cover design for an album called "Come & Gone" by Mason Proffit. Linda, on the other hand, landed a part in a David McCallum thriller called *Dogs* (1976). Unfortunately, her character is mauled to death by a pack of wild dogs at the end of the film.

She also appeared in a 1977 made-for-TV movie, "Murder in Peyton Place." This feature was based on the 1960s TV series "Peyton Place," and included several of the show's original cast members, most notably Dorothy Malone.

Soon afterward, Linda landed one of the more bizarre roles in her career, in the short-lived Norman Lear series called "All That Glitters." The part Gray played on the show was that of transsexual model Linda Murkland. She remembers that the part "was really terribly controversial. Nobody wanted me to do it, but I did it anyway."

She especially remembers explaining the role of Linda Murkland to her mom. "A lot of women had been interviewed for the role, but when I walked in, Norman Lear said, 'You're perfect for the part.' I didn't know whether to laugh or cry. I'll never forget calling my mother. 'I'm finally going to do a series, Mom.' 'That's wonderful, dear, just so you're nice and very pretty.' 'Well, Mom, I'm very nice and very pretty, but I don't know how to quite . . .'" In spite of everyone's opposition, at that time Linda looked upon the part as her greatest challenge.

"Norman assured me I'd be a perfect transsexual," laughs Linda. "He even imported one from San Francisco to coach me. It was unnerving, but I kept thinking, 'How can it be that bad?' I was scared to death, and so was she, but it worked out beautifully.

I learned everything there is to know about the operations involved and the difficult psychological adjustments."

The premise behind the show was that all of the action took place in a society where the men are the housekeepers and secretaries, and the women are the executives running everything. Also in the cast were Lois Nettleton, Jessica Walter, and Anita Gillette. The show unfortunately ran only from April 18 to July 15 of 1977. But for Linda, the experience of doing a regular television series was valuable. It ultimately helped to prepare her for what was to be a huge breakthrough for her in the near future.

Linda's next role was opposite Carol Burnett and Charles Grodin in another television film, "The Grass Is Always Greener Over The Septic Tank" (1978). The movie was based on the best-selling book of the same name, which was written by housewife/humorist Erma Bombeck. In the movie Linda played the part of Leslie, a flirtatious housewife in the neighborhood where Burnett and Grodin have moved. In one scene, Linda sashays over to Grodin at a party and tells him that he has the same "cute but repressed look" that her college sweetheart had. She bats her eyelashes, and Burnett gives her a I'm-going-to-rip-your-face-off look. In another scene Gray is seen at a PTA meeting, dishing the dirt with the other mothers.

Originally this TV movie was intended as a pilot for a proposed weekly series. Unfortunately, the series never transpired.

With each new acting assignment Linda felt that she was coming closer and closer to something substantial. Although these roles in the TV movies were only supporting characters, she knew that she was working with top-notch people, and her turn at success would surely come if she kept trying and didn't give up.

"People said, 'You've got to be crazy, waiting around . . . waiting around for a part to come,'" remembers Linda. "Many of my friends said, 'To hell with it, we're gonna open up a boutique.' But I kept hanging in, and they kept laughing at me. They said, 'You've got to be kidding. You've got two kids, and you're still waiting for the right part.' I don't know whether it was hardheadedness or stubbornness or just masochism, but I just kept hanging in."

★ 4 ★

Enter:
Sue Ellen

The idea that grew into the TV show called "Dallas" began as the brainchild of a writer named David Jacobs. He was the story editor on the popular dramatic series called "Family," and he longed to create a new series that was intriguing, and different.

When Jacobs approached Mike Filerman of Lorimar Productions in 1977, he proposed a television series that would have the human interest impact of Ingmar Bergman's "Scenes from a Marriage" (1973). Bergman originally created "Scenes" as a six-part TV mini-series starring Liv Ullman, and it was later edited into a 168 minute feature film. "Scenes from a Marriage" was a stark, passionate, and moving look at the demise of a Swedish married couple's relationship and the emotional struggles that resulted from their break-up.

But Mike had something a little different in mind—

something along the lines of a 1957 film called *No Down Payment*, a trashy story about adultery in the American suburbs, starring Joanne Woodward and Jeffrey Hunter. *No Down Payment* is sheer soap opera from beginning to end: so-called "respectable" people who attend church every Sunday and cheat on their spouses the rest of the week. Greed, lust, and hedonism—larger than life themes everyone can be fascinated with.

From the melding of these two diverse cinematic formats came the genesis of what ultimately became "Dallas": adult drama played out through the sleazy goings-on in the lives of an urban family. If that didn't sell deodorant and laundry detergent, nothing would!

The show that Jacobs and Filerman originally presented to CBS, like "Scenes from a Marriage," dealt mainly with one couple and took place in an average American suburb like the one in *No Down Payment*. They called their show concept "Knots Landing." CBS liked the idea, but they wanted something bigger, lusher, more monied, and more of a family "saga." David and Mike went back to the drawing board and came up with the perfect setting for their melodrama: Dallas, Texas—the home of the oil business, where fortunes are made by luck and held onto by intelligence.

Jacobs took a couple of his "Knots Landing" characters, Gary and Val Ewing, and set out to expand their family tree to include their rich Texas relatives. CBS wanted a "saga," and Jacobs delivered the perfect family saga. The characters were a cross between the real-life Kennedys and the kind of characters who peopled the film *Giant* (1956). This is what the network considered a highly fascinating concept, and commissioned five episodes, to go into production immediately.

The Ewings are hardly your typical American family. First of all, each member is personally worth an average of $10 million, and they divvy up shares in their family's oil company greedily, as if it were some sort of pie. On each episode of the show, members of the Ewing clan typically enact at least five of the seven deadly sins, for all to see—in vivid living color.

Who could have guessed that the show would end up running ten television seasons, or that at its height of popularity it would be viewed by an estimated 350 million people in fifty-seven different countries! Nevertheless, that was precisely what was to happen.

When Linda Gray showed up for a routine casting call for the show in late 1977, she had no idea what she was getting herself involved in. She had spoken of having been waiting for "the right part" to come along in her acting career . . . and this would be it!

What she was about to become a part of was destined to make TV history. Never before had there been a network-produced prime-time evening soap opera with a continuous plot. "Dallas" was the original. "Dynasty," "Falcon Crest," "The Colbys," and "Knots Landing" all came afterward—after "Dallas" showed them the way.

The scenario for the original five episodes had a plotted course. David Jacobs himself wrote episodes one and five, and three different writers were hired to pen the action for episodes two, three, and four.

In episode one, entitled "Digger's Daughter," the action centers on Bobby Ewing and his young and pretty bride of two hours, Pamela Barnes Ewing. Pam is the daughter of the Ewings' rival, Digger Barnes, who has thrown his life away by trying to drown his sorrows in a whiskey bottle. The main conflict of the first episode centers on the characters of Pam, and Bobby's brother J.R. The idea was to have Bobby killed off in episode five and to leave his widowed bride Pam as the show's leading protagonist, with J.R. as the antagonist. From the very beginning it was intended that Pam and J.R. would carry the entire show, and everyone else would be supporting characters. The character of J.R.'s wife, Sue Ellen, was barely fleshed out in the first five episodes when casting began.

The first person to be cast was Barbara Bel Geddes, as the family matriarch Eleanor Ewing, fondly known as Miss Ellie. Next came Jim Davis as her husband, John Ross ("Jock") Ewing I. Patrick Duffy, fresh from the series "The Man From Atlantis," was cast as Bobby Ewing.

The casting choices for the other characters were as yet undecided. The role of J.R. was up between Larry Hagman and Robert Foxworth. As we know, Hagman became the infamous J.R., and Foxworth went on to become one of the stars of "Falcon Crest" as Chase Gioberti. The choice for the role of Pam was narrowed down to Judith Chapman and Victoria Principal; Principal ultimately won the part.

Some people ended up being cast in roles other than the ones that they originally auditioned for. In the beginning Ken Kercheval tried out for the role of Ray Krebbs, and Steve Kanaly was one of the people who had read Bobby's part. Kercheval was ultimately cast as Cliff Barnes, and Kanaly was given the role of Ray Krebbs.

Next came the choice for the actress to play J.R.

Ewing's wife, Sue Ellen. When Linda auditioned for the part of Sue Ellen, she was one of thirty actresses up for that role. For her try-out, the script had only four lines for Sue Ellen, and it called for her to become upset afterwards. Linda Gray had only one shot at the audition, so she figured she'd give it her all. Instead of just getting depressed at the end of the dialogue, she decided to really break down and cry. "I said to myself, 'Just let it go!' Tears flowed," Linda remembers. "And the producers were sitting there, as if saying, 'How did you do that?' I said, 'That's called acting!'"

The producers were impressed, and she was called back for the part. They finally narrowed their casting decision down to two actresses for the role of Sue Ellen. It was either going to go to Linda Gray or to Mary Frann. Ultimately they decided to hire Linda. Mary Frann eventually went on to TV fame for her portrayal of Bob Newhart's wife Joanna on the show "Newhart."

Although she had been hired for this impressive new show, Linda nearly went into shock when she found out how little she had to do on camera. "It was the damnedest thing," Linda recalls. "In the first episode, I had about two lines, like 'More coffee, dear?' And though I was supposed to be the wife of another then-minor character named J.R., there was nothing in the script to indicate *what* I was to him—secretary, mistress, maybe even just a tennis partner! The main story was a modern Romeo-Juliet version of Bobby Ewing, the rich kid, having this heavy romance with Pam, the poor girl from across the tracks. It was all Patrick Duffy and Victoria Principal. Most of the rest of the cast were little more than supernumeraries."

One of the show's casting directors, Ruth Conorte,

later admitted, "All we wanted for the 'Dallas' casting in those hectic days was kind of a walk-on actress who could look as if she once had been a Miss Texas in the Miss America contest."

According to the show's producer, Leonard Katzman, "I guess we just didn't realize the gold mine we had. Larry Hagman had come from sitcom: 'I Dream Of Jeannie'; Linda hadn't done much of anything. From the very first show, it was his genius and *her* instinct that made J.R. and Sue Ellen the more dominant characters. He created the smiling villain for himself. She didn't have many lines, so she did most of her acting with those astounding eyes of hers. Just listening to Larry tell of one of his evil deeds, her facial reactions indicated Sue Ellen was a character with a great range of emotions—understanding her husband's villainy, but caught in a lust-sick relationship that had her go along with him. She certainly saw much more in the character than we did when we started."

"I'm sure I got the job because of my looks [more] than anything else," Linda says of her first days on the show. "Larry had these wonderful evil lines, and I remember looking at him and thinking, 'I'm supposed to be married to this guy and he's such a jerk! Who would marry him?' The lady who would marry him would have to have a few things going on with her psychologically. So I decided that she was not terribly together. When they shot my close-up, I did something with my eyes that said more than words could say. They saw it in the dailies and started writing for it."

However, things were not absolutely perfect from the very start. Larry and Linda had a huge altercation right after their first dialogue was filmed. "I had to tell her she was terrible after our first scene together!" claims Hagman.

Linda distinctly recalls, "Larry threw me in his van after it was over. He yelled at me, 'Get in there! I want to talk to you!' I was totally intimidated. Then he said, 'That scene is the first one that CBS will see of us as Sue Ellen and J.R., and you were terrible!'" After that Hagman and Gray simply worked out their differences and went on with the show. They eventually became best friends. Somehow things began to click for Larry and Linda on screen, and from that point forward, their on-screen time grew and grew.

The first five episodes were shot entirely on location in Texas. For Linda, this was the first time that she had spent that much time away from Ed and the kids. It was a strain, but in retrospect it was a positive time for all four of them. They all grew as individuals.

"When we filmed the mini-series," explains Gray, "we spent two months in Dallas. Ed was here [in Los Angeles] burning pork chops for the children. That was the first time there was no mommy. I don't care what kind of marriage you have, that puts a strain on it. I spent my salary on airplane tickets home. That was also the first time I was alone, and as delightful as it was at first, listening to what I wanted and no responsibilities, I didn't know how to be alone. I went from 'Mom' and 'Dad' to 'husband.' I thought, 'My God, here I am by myself!' It was not only a growing experience for me, but also a wonderful way for Ed and the kids to realize what I was in this family. It was great for everybody, but at the moment nobody realized the greatness of it all."

The first five episodes of "Dallas" were the crucial

ones. Would people tune in again week after week to find out what was happening to the characters introduced in episode one? The all-important Nielsen ratings would decide everyone's fate.

The initial five episodes of "Dallas" aired on consecutive Sunday nights. The first episode, "Digger's Daughter," was used to establish the characters and their continuing conflicts. When Bobby and Pam arrive at the Ewing's ranch, South Fork, and announce that they've just eloped and are now man and wife, the greetings they receive are less than warm. Instead of patching up the feud between the Barnes and Ewing families, both sides vow to rekindle the war that had started in 1930. Until that time Jock Ewing (John Ross Ewing I) had been Digger Barnes' business partner. Now that Jock is rolling in money, and Digger is a hopeless sot, their heirs have decided to continue the fight.

From the word go, J.R. enacts the first of the dastardly deeds that would become his trademark. First he offers Pam a cash settlement to annul her marriage. When she refuses, he decides to take more drastic measures. He plots to have Bobby stumble in on Pam in the arms of her former lover—the South Fork ranch hand Ray Krebbs.

But clever Pam sees through J.R.'s staged event and blackmails Ray: if he won't admit to Bobby that the whole thing was an underhanded scheme by J.R. to break up their marriage, she'll reveal Ray's secret affair with the Ewing brothers' teenage niece, Lucy. By the end of episode one, it is clear that there is stormy weather ahead for the whole family, as Pam's brother Cliff Barnes swears to destroy the entire Ewing empire.

As you can see, there isn't a single curve in the plot that in any way involves Sue Ellen. Gray was quite accurate when she proclaimed that, "For the first couple of 'Dallas' shows my lines ran to 'More coffee?' and 'I have a headache.'"

The second episode, called "Lessons," centered on young Lucy, who has been skipping school to learn about the birds and the bees—in bed with Ray. Lucy (actress Charlene Tilton) has been intercepting the truancy letters sent by the school. When someone from the school calls South Fork to find out Lucy's whereabouts, Pam intercepts the call.

Pam puts two and two together and decides to confront "bad girl" Lucy. Catching Ray and Lucy in a compromising position, she cons Lucy into returning to school by threatening to report the incident to the family. Lucy, however, conspires to make Pam's well-meaning act backfire by staging a scene to make it appear that she's been sexually assulted by one of the school's counselors.

"Spy in the House" was episode three. It centers around Cliff Barnes, who is sleeping with J.R.'s secretary, Julie Gray (actress Tina Louise), to gain valuable information about the Ewings. Cliff comes up with some incriminating documents that suggest that the Ewings have been involved in shady business dealings with a state senator.

J.R. in turn accuses Pam of having turned the documents over to her brother, Cliff, and of having married Bobby only to spy on the family. When Bobby discovers that J.R. has also been sleeping with Julie, he unravels the mystery of the incriminating documents. He in turn blackmails J.R.: If J.R. doesn't leave Pam alone, he'll tell Sue Ellen about his affair with the secretary.

In the fourth episode, "Winds of Vengeance," Sue Ellen finally comes into the spotlight. When Luther Frick (actor Brian Dennehy) discovers his wife in a cheap motel room in Waco, Texas, he flies into a rage. When he finds one of J.R.'s business cards in her possession, he vows to get even with the Ewings.

A tornado blows into Dallas, and in the ensuing confusion, Frick and one of his cronies force their way into South Fork. The inhabitants of the house include J.R., Ray, and the Ewing women. Frick's plan is to tie up the men and force them to watch their women being gang raped. Sue Ellen is forced at gunpoint to put on her swimsuit and "Miss Texas" sash from the 1968 Miss America contest. It seems that Frick is most turned on by the idea of raping Miss Texas before a captive audience. Faced with this horror, Sue Ellen, clad only in her strapless one-piece bathing suit and a little butterfly pendant on a gold chain, breaks down and cries hysterically. This scene gave Linda a chance to use the effective crying-on-cue acting technique that originally won her the role.

Naturally, the planned gang rape backfires, and Frick is taken into custody. When Bobby returns to South Fork, Pam relates to him how awful the whole scene was but proudly adds that everyone banded together as a family in the face of the ordeal. At long last Linda Gray's character was being used in a more exciting way: no longer merely the shy housewife who serves coffee to her husband.

In episode five, which was called "Barbecue," the intention was to set up the type of family conflict that would leave audiences wanting to see further episodes of the show to discover the outcome. The setting was the Ewing's annual family barbecue. Pam seizes the moment to make the happy announcement that she is pregnant. This is all Sue Ellen needs for an excuse to confront J.R. She lets him know that he is destined to fail at the simplest task—namely, creating a male heir for the family fortune. She hammers away on the fact that Pam and Bobby have beaten them to the punch. Since Sue Ellen and J.R. have been childless for the past eight years, she makes certain that he is aware that Bobby will become—now more evidently than ever—Jock's favorite son.

J.R. walks over to Bobby and makes the insinuation that Pam's child has probably been fathered by Ray. When J.R. follows Pam into a hayloft in the barn, Pam begins fighting physically with him, and falls onto a lower loft below. The force of her fall causes Pam to suffer a miscarriage.

At the end of the show, Bobby vows to leave South Fork and never return. Jock tries to make peace, and Miss Ellie goes into a "where-did-I-go-wrong?" monologue.

The fifth show left all sorts of cliffhanger plot elements to be resolved—if the show was a success, and production resumed. Would Pam ever be able to have children after her accident? Would Sue Ellen and J.R. produce an offspring out of spite? Would Cliff Barnes make good on his vow to destroy the Ewings? Would Lucy get caught in bed with Ray? Had J.R. turned Bobby against the family?

After the fifth show had aired on April 30, 1978, the executives at CBS took a look at the ratings figures that the shows had drawn. Three of the episodes had scored over a thirty share of the viewing audience, and one of the episodes—"Barbecue"—was in the Top Ten ratings for the day on which it aired. Here was all the evidence that the network needed, and it was announced that "Dallas" would indeed return that fall. CBS gave the go-ahead for thirteen more episodes of "Dallas," and so began a piece of television history.

It was in those next thirteen episodes that the part of Sue Ellen really began to develop. The more the producers of the show saw of Linda's capabilities, the more they wrote into the script for her to do. According to Leonard Katzman, "We were looking for a beautiful lady, but at that point we thought of Sue Ellen as all polish and no brains. That she's evolved into a character of depth and dimension is all because of Linda. The more we saw her, the more we knew she could do and the wider she stretched."

It was five shows into the 1978–1979 season that Sue Ellen's real build up began. The episode was entitled "Black Market Baby." Worried that Pam and Bobby will again conceive the next Ewing heir, Sue Ellen decides to take matters into her own hands. She gets the idea into her head to adopt a baby so that, even if Pam does become pregnant, her child will be the first of Jock Ewing's grandchildren.

When Sue Ellen discovers that legitimate adoption services take longer than she is willing to wait, she turns to an illegal "black market" source. Sue Ellen agrees to pay $15,000 to an unwed mother for her baby. But when she and the mother are out on a shopping spree for the baby, who do they run into at the store . . . but Pam. Pam had worked at the store before she married Bobby, and that very afternoon she is attempting to get her old job back.

Pam in turn confronts Sue Ellen about her obvious

race to have the first child in the family. Although Sue Ellen is certain that Pam will blackmail her with this revelation, she does not. However, J.R. does get wind of what his wife is up to, and he puts an end to her whole scheme of purchasing a child.

It is in the ninth episode of the first season of "Dallas" that Sue Ellen's famous drinking problem is revealed. It was a theme that was to become an issue throughout the run of the show. The episode was entitled "Survival." In it, J.R. and Bobby are traveling in the small airplane their family owns, when it crashes in a swamp. Because of a severe thunderstorm, the local authorities cannot reach the downed craft for several hours, and are uncertain whether the Ewing brothers have survived the crash or not. Meanwhile, back at the ranch, their wives are wringing their hands with worry.

While Pam verbally contemplates the emptiness of her life without her beloved Bobby, Sue Ellen mentions her concern over not conceiving a Ewing baby. Bitchy Lucy takes advantage of the looming tragedy to lash out at Sue Ellen. She proclaims that Sue Ellen isn't really concerned about J.R.'s well-being, she's just worried that she has blown her chance at a legitimate stake in the South Fork ranch . . . a stake that Sue Ellen could only have claimed by producing a child. Sue Ellen is shaken by Lucy's callous comment and heads straight for the bottle.

Of course, J.R. and Bobby return home safely. It seems that it was J.R. who bravely pulled them out of the swamp. Unfortunately, Sue Ellen was never to win a complete victory over her drinking problem from that point on; in times of great stress the temptation of the bottle would always be there. It became her signature weakness, one that was played upon heavily in the show.

On the day of the crash, while J.R.'s whereabouts are unknown, Sue Ellen has been flirting with her husband's archrival, Cliff Barnes (actor Ken Kercheval. In the next episode, "Act Of Love," Sue Ellen takes things a step further and begins a full-fledged affair with Barnes. It seems that Cliff flatters her and builds up her ego—something that J.R. hasn't done in years. Later in the episode, Sue Ellen finds out that she's at long last pregnant. But whose child is she carrying—Cliff's or J.R.'s?

Later in the season, Sue Ellen's greedy sister Kristin (actress Mary Crosby) shows up in Dallas with their meddling mother, Patricia Shepard (actress Martha Scott). They are driving Sue Ellen crazy. Finally, fed up with J.R.'s string of cheap affairs, she resumes her own affair with Cliff. Amoral Cliff in turn tries to use his liason with Sue Ellen to secure damaging information about J.R.

Meanwhile, the other characters on "Dallas" have been having their own personal traumas as well. Bobby has been kidnapped. Jock survives a heart attack. Miss Ellie's long-lost brother comes home to die. Lucy's mother, Valene, is banished forever from South Fork. Pam is framed by J.R. and a former-hooker, ex-girlfriend of his, and her photo appears on the front page of the local morning newspaper, which identifies her as a prostitute. Cliff Barnes loses his bid at becoming a state senator—thanks to J.R.'s smear campaign. J.R.'s secretary, Julie, is found stealing Ewing confidential information and falls to her death while being pursued by his henchmen. After an affair with a country singer, Ray Krebbs falls in love with Donna Mc-

Cullum Culver (actress Susan Howard). And, Lucy falls in love with Kit Mainwaring III, only to find out that he is gay.

By the end of that first season, the show had already experienced its first, change of actors as the part of Digger Barnes, originally played by David Wayne, was taken over by Keenan Wynn. However, stretches of the imagination such as this are the stuff on which all television soap operas must depend from time to time.

In the spring of 1979, it came time to wrap up the first season of "Dallas," with the series' first precedent-setting "cliffhanger." Never before in television history had a series left an important matter unresolved and kept the viewers waiting until the following autumn for the denouement.

Fortunately for Linda Gray, the first season's cliffhanger involved Sue Ellen. It was a suspenseful plot twist that was carefully constructed over the final two episodes of the first season.

In the episode entitled "John Ewing III, Part One," we find that Sue Ellen's drinking problem has gotten totally out of hand. Even her mother-in-law and father-in-law, Miss Ellie and Jock, cannot ignore the fact that she is becoming a major-league alcoholic. Besides that, she is carrying their unborn grandchild. The Ewings decide that they must take action, and J.R. is ultimately forced to commit Sue Ellen to a sanitarium to dry out.

In the next and final episode of the season, "John Ewing III, Part Two," we find Sue Ellen in residence at the elite Fletcher Sanitarium, against her will. In a tearful confession, Sue Ellen tells her problems to Bobby, underlining the fact that she is convinced that the baby she is carrying is actually Cliff's.

Sue Ellen feels like a caged animal in the sanitarium, but a consoling Bobby implores her to allow the staff to help her with her dependence on booze. J.R. shows up for a visit, and gloatingly shows her a photo from the local newspaper of Cliff Barnes with his new girlfriend. This pushes Sue Ellen over the edge: she has to have a drink immediately. After bribing one of the nurses, she has liquor smuggled in to her, disguised as bottles of mouthwash. Later she escapes from the sanitarium and tries to flee in her car, only to end up in a traffic accident.

Moments before her car bursts into flames, Sue Ellen is dragged to safety. At Dallas Memorial Hospital, the doctors discover that if they do not act fast, she will lose her baby. They perform an immediate cesarean section. The baby is not due to be delivered for a full eight weeks; will it survive? And if it does, who is the real father? For the matter, will Sue Ellen survive her injuries from the accident? That is how the first season of "Dallas" ended.

Linda Gray especially remembers filming the scenes depicting her pregnancy. Naturally, the "baby" that she was carrying for those episodes was nothing more than padding. "A gradual progression of changing funny pillows," is how she describes her TV maternity. She laughingly recounts, "I kept forgetting 'the baby.' I'd leave it in my dressing room, and one time I even left it in a phone booth. I felt like a terrible mother even before I had it!"

As that first season progressed, Linda was discovering who Sue Ellen Ewing was, in terms of how she would walk, dress, eat, and carry herself. "I went back to my old acting class notes and decided that, because of her background, Sue Ellen would never be sloppy.

I wouldn't over do it: she'd be a sophisticated rummy," she claims. Discussing the sharp contrast between Sue Ellen and the real-life Linda Gray, she goes on, "Sue Ellen wears silk, and I'm a tomboy in blue jeans. I'm big on Perrier water and shoveling horse manure." Can you imagine Sue Ellen Ewing in the barn with a shovel in her hand? Never!

"She is totally unpredictable," continues Linda about Sue Ellen, "and I think that's why she fascinates the viewers. She married J.R. in the first place for money and power. Her mother wanted her to be Miss Texas in order to catch the eye of the richest man in Texas. But Mom forgot to tell her about emotions. So, Sue Ellen is in the throes of finding out what she is going to do with her life. She's a woman in conflict, and other women, who are trying to decide what to do with their lives, can relate to that. I get letters from many women, not necessarily from Texas, but from all over who identify with the character."

As that first season progressed, and Linda's importance in the show grew, she found that she was enjoying it more and more. "I'm doing exactly what I want to now!" she happily proclaimed at the time.

Linda especially liked the sense of camaraderie that developed on the set of the television show. She and Larry Hagman became best buddies almost immediately. "I think Larry is fabulous, as a human being, and as an actor, and as everything!" she exclaimed after her first season on the show.

Likewise, Hagman admitted, "When Linda and I work together, the sparks fly. She plays Sue Ellen with a smoldering sexiness coupled with an innocent bitchiness that just intrigues people."

According to Charlene Tilton, who portrays Lucy on

the show, "She plays a drunk with such elegance that you feel for her even when she's almost killing her baby or lying in a ditch! [She's] warm, funny, and very, very generous."

One of the more strained relationships on the set was that between Linda Gray and Victoria Principal. In the original premise of the show, Victoria's character, Pam Ewing was supposed to be *the* lead female character. By the end of the season, the character of Sue Ellen was gaining prominence and importance, and Linda was getting more and more screen time.

Explained Linda, "We have a pleasant relationship, but the situation must be hard on Victoria, and there has to be some resentment."

However, Victoria had only complimentary words for Linda when she was asked to comment. According to her, "[Linda] can act anyone right off the floor. She is so in touch with her own emotions and priorities."

Even more important for Linda was the impact that being in a regular series made on her personal life. While a lot of the interior filming does take place in the Los Angeles area, the exterior shots of Dallas, and many of the scenes at the South Fork ranch, are shot in Texas. That meant spending much of her time each year out of town, away from her family.

According to Linda, as her work load increased, she and Ed worked out things so that she could have the best of both her career and her home life. "When the series was picked up and we had to go back to Dallas for more filming, we did a wonderful thing with the kids. By then they hated each other, so I brought each down separately with a friend for a two-week visit. They went to the set and out to dinner. They were in heaven," she recalls.

During the time that she was in California, she also worked out a schedule to spend quality time with her son and daughter. "We developed a wonderful thing," she explains. "I promise to spend two hours a week with each one, away from home, and we do something each wants to do. The time has to be mutually agreed, and I've got a calendar with my schedule on the refrigerator. Kehly loves to shop. I took Jeff trap-shooting one Sunday. One weekend, he chose to go skiing with friends, and he had to forfeit his time, but he chose to do it. That's called growing up and being responsible. When you have a deal, it makes a lot of people grow up real fast.

"By my doing what you know and believe is best for you, you can do beautiful things for those around you. The most important gift you can give a child is the example of the pleasure and satisfaction of doing what you want wholeheartedly. When they decide what they want to do, I hope I've given them that modeling role."

As an actress, Linda was really feeling challenged unlike any other time in her life. "A TV series is terribly demanding," she admitted. "There are times when I have my big crying scene, and we have seven minutes before they break for lunch or go into meal penalty [union-defined mealtime that must be adhered to or fines have to be paid]. You have to dig deep down and hope you can get it in the next seven minutes. But I love working under pressure. Something magical happens when you're down to the wire.

"The only problem with doing 'Dallas,'" Linda explained, "is that it has meant a total readjustment to my life. I have to be at the studio which is an hour's drive from home, by 5:30 A.M., and I am seldom finished before six or seven in the evening, six days a week. It has made me learn to make every moment of my life count. I love to cook and I like to eat. Therefore, I am always on a diet. Now I cook only when time permits, which usually means I am running around the kitchen desperately trying to throw anything I can find into a dish because I'm home late from the studio.

"I also love going to the gymnasium, although I find I have little time for that as well. I spend as much time as possible working on toning and slimming machines. I also jog whenever possible. To be honest, I don't really like jogging. But I love it when I stop—it feels so good. I love to swim, ski, play tennis and ride horses. I have to be outside in whatever I do. Sue Ellen wouldn't understand this kind of life!"

For Linda Gray, those first seasons on "Dallas" meant her arrival at the kind of life that she had always imagined. She had her career, her family, and was in a hit TV series. Everything was just going onward and upward from that point on, and she was loving every minute of it. After Sue Ellen Ewing entered her life, things were never to be the same as they were before.

★ 5 ★

Stardom on "Dallas"

The 1979–1980 season of "Dallas" undoubtedly became one of the most famous years in its illustrious history. It was that season that ended with the most unforgettable cliffhanger of them all: "Who shot J.R.?" The bullet that left J.R. Ewing bleeding on the floor of his office at Ewing Oil was truly the 1980s version of "the shot heard 'round the world." For Linda Gray and several of her colleagues, this was the season that catapulted them to international stardom.

In addition to her work on "Dallas" that year, Linda appeared in the first of several made-for-TV movies which she filmed during her annual breaks between seasons of the nighttime soap opera. "The Two Worlds of Jennie Logan" (1979) offered Linda a chance for a departure from her weekly role as the often tipsy Sue Ellen Ewing.

The film starred Lindsay Wagner as Jennie Logan, a

modern-day New York City housewife who moves with her husband to an old New England town. The grand old house they move into has been vacant for several years, and many of the original inhabitants' possessions still remain untouched. The dusty attic is filled with memorabilia from the late 1890s, left by the original owners of the house.

Among the odds and ends Jennie finds there is a lace dress from the turn of the century. As a lark, she has the dress cleaned and restored, only to find that whenever she wears it, she is able to transport herself back in time, to the era in which the dress was first worn.

Suddenly finding herself in the yard of the same house—in 1899—she is mistaken for a woman who has just died. She establishes the fact that she is not the dead woman's ghost, but soon finds herself falling in love with the handsome and romantic widower, played by actor Marc Singer. Singer plays the part of artist David Reynolds, a man who is far more exciting and understanding than Jennie's real-life husband.

Although she prefers her 1890s lover to her 1970s husband, Jennie encounters further complications in the past. Through historical research she does in 1979, she discovers that the man she loves in 1899 is going to be murdered on a certain night. This is where Linda Gray comes in, as Elizabeth Harrington, who is also in love with David.

Jennie decides that she is going to solve the murder, save David's life, and then decide whether to continue her life in the present with a husband she does not trust or with the man in 1899 with whom she has finally found happiness. While researching the case further in the archives of the local library in 1979,

Jennie comes across a reference to a local 103-year-old citizen, whom everyone in town fondly refers to as "Aunt Betty." Could she actually be Elizabeth Harrington? It turns out that she is indeed and that she holds the secret to the 1899 murder that Jennie intends to solve—and prevent.

The movie is quite intriguing, and it was especially enjoyable for Linda Gray to appear in. It offered her several new challenges as an actress; she relished the chance to play the character of Elizabeth, both as a young turn-of-the-century belle and as an old woman.

"I got an opportunity to age from twenty-eight to a hundred and three," Linda explains. "I hired Robert Easton, who helped me with the Dallas accent, to help me with the old-lady voice. It was a challenge, and I'd rather go for the challenge. I'm going for the long term. I don't want to be just an overnight TV star. You know, I'm a great believer that you can do anything you want to do if you have all the perseverance in the world."

In the 1979–1980 season on "Dallas," Linda found that her role of Sue Ellen continued to gain more prominence in the plot. The more work that the producers of the show gave her, the more she grew as an actress. "It was a lovely compliment that they recognized I was able to do something more," she proudly admitted.

The new season opened with Sue Ellen in the hospital, still recovering from the traffic accident. However, she finds herself feeling like the rope in an emotional tug-of-war. J.R. reassures Sue Ellen that she will soon be home at South Fork, while Cliff Barnes argues that she should move in with him, since he is convinced that the baby is his.

J.R. insists that Sue Ellen return to South Fork to regain her strength, while the premature baby, John Ross III, remains in the hospital under constant supervision. Everyone at South Fork is concerned about Sue Ellen's health. She seems lethargic and unconcerned about life. Will she snap out of her trance or not?

When Sue Ellen and J.R. return to the hospital several days later to pick up the baby, they discover—much to their horror—that he has been kidnapped! Naturally, Cliff Barnes is the prime suspect. However, in the following episode it is revealed that the kidnapper is actually a deranged woman who lost her own baby in childbirth. John Ross III ends up back at South Fork, but only after a great deal of trauma for the Ewings.

By the fourth episode of the season, Sue Ellen's younger sister, the lusty Kristin, begins having an affair with J.R. Since Sue Ellen isn't interested in J.R., Kristin feels no guilt in keeping her brother-in-law happy. Meanwhile, Cliff Barnes brings his father, Digger, to Dallas to help him with his plan to destroy the Ewings. Digger is in need of a doctor, and it is revealed that he is dying from a genetic disorder known as neurofibromatosis. If John Ross III is actually Cliff's son, he stands a good chance of inheriting the illness, and dying suddenly.

Unable to get her life in order, Sue Ellen decides to seek psychiatric help. However, she doesn't want the family to find out, so she sees the doctor secretly. In the seventh episode of the season, appropriately entitled "Rodeo," Sue Ellen renews her acquaintance with a sexy local cowboy named Dusty Farlow (actor Jared Martin), at the annual Ewing Rodeo. Suddenly

Sue Ellen regains the will to live. The new romance gives her a new lease on life!

Meanwhile, Pam discovers that she is pregnant again. She is really excited about it until she talks to her brother Cliff, who tells her about the illness that is killing Digger, and she realizes that she may be passing the deadly disease on to her unborn child. But Pam falls off of her horse while out riding and suffers her second miscarriage. After that, Pam is convinced that the risk of the disease is too great for her to consider giving birth, and she resigns herself to a life without children.

Amid all this activity, Sue Ellen finds she simply can't get into her new role as mother. When the baby cries, she ignores him. It is Pam who eventually responds to the child's needs. By giving John Ross III affection, she finds it easier to bear the fact that she cannot have children of her own.

While all of this is going on, Miss Ellie makes a couple of startling discoveries. First she finds a lump in one of her breasts, and later she unearths the fact that Jock has been married once before—something he has never told her about. The first Mrs. Ewing had become mentally ill and is still living in an institution. When Jock found out about her illness, he divorced her and pretended that she never existed. This revelation, coupled with her medical problem causes real trauma for Miss Ellie. She gets medical help and finds she does indeed require a mastectomy.

In the sexual affairs department: Lucy falls in love with a lawyer named Alan Beam (actor Randolph Powell). J.R.'s affair with Kristin hits full swing, while Sue Ellen is enjoying her afternoon trysts with Dusty Farlow in a local motel. And, finally, by mid-season both J.R. and Cliff submit to blood tests, which reveal that Sue Ellen's child is indeed a Ewing.

During all of these goings-on, Pam is busy with her retail job and leaves Dallas on a business trip to Paris. Just as she leaves town, Bobby's old sweetheart Jenna Wade shows up. (During this particular season, the role of Jenna is played by actress Francine Tacker.) At one point in the season it looks as if both Pam and Sue Ellen will divorce the Ewing brothers. Bobby is coming dangerously close to a fling with Jenna, Sue Ellen is sleeping with Dusty, and J.R. and Kristin are going at it hot and heavy.

Sue Ellen asks J.R. for a divorce, and he agrees, as long as she leaves their son behind at South Fork. When Sue Ellen suddenly starts to behave as if their marriage were going perfectly, J.R. plots to make her return to drinking so that he can prove that she is an unfit mother, and is therefore due a smaller divorce settlement.

When a long-decaying body is unearthed on South Fork, it turns out to be the corpse of Hutch McKinney, the ex-foreman of the ranch. Since Hutch had disappeared on the day that Jock had fired him, Jock is the prime suspect in the case, and he ends up in jail for murder.

Sue Ellen decides to run away from the Ewings. However when Dusty fails to show up for one of their rendezvous, she reacquaints herself with the liquor bottle—thus playing right into J.R.'s hands. Unfortunately for the emotionally fragile Sue Ellen, she later learns that Dusty was out flying in his private plane and crashed. However, his remains were not positively identified. The mystery is still unsolved: is he dead or alive? This drives poor Sue Ellen into an even deeper depression. Has she lost her only chance at happiness? That question would remain unanswered until the following autumn.

The season winds up with its most explosive episode—"The House Divided." In it, just about everyone has a motive for wanting J.R. dead. In the final scene, when J.R. is shot by an unknown assailant, there are numerous suspects.

Cliff Barnes has just discovered that his father, Digger, who has just died, was originally Jock's fifty-fifty partner in Ewing Oil, and J.R. has surpressed the evidence. J.R. wants Kristin out of the way, so he has her arrested for prostitution. When she is arrested, the sheriff agrees to give her twenty-four hours to leave town. When Alan Beam purchases a gun, he appears to have reasonable motives as well. J.R. has just finished cheating several of his business partners out of a lucrative Asian oil deal, and they all want him dead. Bobby is disgusted with J.R. for his underhanded dealings, and announces that he is leaving South Fork. Even Miss Ellie claims she'll never forgive him for breaking up her family. And—last but not least—J.R. has sworn to commit Sue Ellen to the sanitarium again. As two shots rang out in J.R.'s office at Ewing Oil that fateful night, all the world wanted to know: "Who shot J.R.?"

The Monday evening before the big cliffhanger episode aired, Linda was one of the stars to be seen on the TV special "Bob Hope In 'The Starmakers.'" The CBS special was an hour-long comedy sketch in which Hope portrayed the part of Miles Bauduc, a talent agent who has fallen onto hard times. Robert Ulrich played a wealthy Texan named Ace Robbins, who teams up with Bauduc to produce a TV series called "Levitt's Lovelies."

In the plot of the comedy teleplay, Linda Gray played Wendy Trousdale, the star of "Levitt's Lovelies." Her co-stars included Bernadette Peters, Robert Guillaume, Elaine Joyce, and comedian Gallager.

By March 21, 1980, when "The House Divided" episode of "Dallas" aired, Linda Gray was already planning her hectic extracurricular schedule. In addition to some global vacationing, she was also set to appear on Australian TV, to shoot another made-for-TV movie, and to take singing lessons in preparation for her musical debut on a Christmas special.

"Dallas" had made her into a star, and Linda was enthralled with her new-found fame. Although new pressures in her personal life accompanied her celebrity status, she glowingly admitted, "Now I'm enjoying it all. The benefits far outnumber the costs. Don't all girls fantasize about becoming a rich and famous actress? Well, it happened to me, and at first I wasn't sure if I should feel guilty about it. But I have finally come to be who I am with no apologies. I have a lot of skinned knees from trying to get to this point, but I've always picked myself up.

"I'm learning to love my celebrity. I love the money. I love all those funny letters from gentlemen who want to come take me away from J.R.!" she laughs. "I never knew what having money was all about. I still don't really. My business manager invests the checks. Do you know what's wonderful about having a business manager? When April rolls around, you don't have to collect those little piles of paper for income taxes. The manager does it. Oh, God, it's heaven!

"I just love playing Sue Ellen," Linda proclaimed after completing the 1979–1980 season on the show. "I think it's just about the best part for a woman on television today. It's such a meaty role. Every time I read a new script, I'm amazed at what she has to go through. I could never get bored with the part—I hope it goes on forever. There is nothing at all of me in Sue Ellen except that, like her, I love to wear pretty clothes. But I feel proud I have created a believable lady who, through all her conflicts, still receives so much empathy from the public. I mean, she is drinking, and she has affairs and does all the things that are totally unacceptable for a woman in society today. So I feel to get all that empathy from women around the world I must be doing something right."

Naturally, for Linda, when her fame really began to blossom, one of her main concerns was how it would affect her children. "We keep a low profile," she said at the time. "The children go to school and live a normal life. Stars today are different than the earlier Hollywood types like Lana Turner. We go on talk shows, and people see we're just like everybody else with the same problems running a home and raising children. We're not walking around dripping diamonds and wearing fur boas.

"When the kids were little, it was very important for me to be a good mommy. I judged myself by that standard. Now, the house is run by committee. I'm terribly proud of the way they've taken over. Kehly went on a talk show with me and was asked if she resented my success, because of the time it took me away from home. She answered that she was very proud of me, that I was doing what I was meant to do. I needed to hear that."

Naturally, becoming a television star brings with it a unique set of pressures. Along with the adulation from the fans comes a suffocating feeling that everyone wants a piece of you. At this point in his wife's career Ed Thrasher explained, "She's very warm and really loves meeting people, but sometimes I have to put them off. My God, we'd have a hundred and eighty people living with us who would all think they were her closest friends."

"For the first couple of years of 'Dallas,' there was a strong adjustment problem for all of us," admitted Linda. "The more successful the series gets, the more everybody wants something from you. Everyone needs some type of outlet to vent their frustrations and work off some of the normal steam and pressure that builds up. I give so much of myself in my part that it is nice to have a retreat where I can totally unwind. Often I do this by working the ranch."

She explained that she usually begins her "un-Dallas-izing" process as soon as she leaves the set each day in her cream-colored Mercedes Benz. "Fortunately, I live an hour away from the studio and on the drive home, my car is my decompression chamber. I roll down my windows and sing at the top of my voice, just to get Sue Ellen out of my system. So by the time I'm home with my husband, two kids, and all the animals, I'm me again. I've thought of moving closer to the studio, but if I did, I might suddenly find myself throwing the china all around the house.

"While I'm working, people are fiddling with my hair and make-up all day long. So, when the weekend comes, I wash my face, pull my hair back, ride my horse to the top of the nearest hill, and contemplate nature. I even have a hammock to rest in. I've heard stories about actors getting hurt by people who were so incensed by their TV roles. But that hasn't happened to me even though I play a mixed-up, bitchy character."

However, by the summer of 1980 things were changing even more quickly than before. While in the past Linda proclaimed that her horse, Granger, was her therapeutic outlet, soon she didn't even have time to devote to him. Later that year Linda reported, "The only star in our family in my horse. I didn't have time to ride him, so I sent him to Lindsay Wagner's stable in Oregon. He has piped-in music, forced-air heat and air conditioning. That horse is *living!*"

The whole "Who shot J.R.?" controversy, and the publicity that went along with it, pushed everyone involved to a new, higher level of visibility. Before the new season began, Linda Gray, Larry Hagman, and Patrick Duffy were all in strong positions to demand salary increases. Not only did Linda's horse take a back seat to her fame, but her husband, Ed, was also beginning to feel a degree of resentment as well.

"At first it was a total jolt for him," Linda admitted. She paralleled her situation with Thrasher to Jon Peters' live-in relationship with Barbra Streisand. "When people called Jon 'Mr. Streisand,' he just freaked out. Well, Ed freaked too. Everybody has an ego. Fortunately, Ed is very secure within himself. We grew up together and struggled. It was not nineteen years of 'Father Knows Best.' And there's no direct conflict. He is not an actor. It could have been devastating. I remember going to the Grammy Awards when he was being nominated for producing album covers. Now he is going to award dinners for me. 'It's My Turn,' as Diana Ross would say. We were all really thrust into this. Ed had to hang on and hope for the best, as our relationship was flipped the other way."

According to Linda, she essentially told her family, "All right, it's my turn now. Hang in there for a while. This won't be forever. It's like your mom has gone to college." She added, "They all had to make adjustments."

Could Linda's marriage withstand the new demands that were being placed on her? When filming for the 1979–1980 "Dallas" season was finished, Linda made her own choices. She could have taken the time off and temporarily resumed the role of housewife for a couple of months. Ed probably would have liked to see her do that. However, she chose to take on several new challenges instead. Her career was important to her. She had worked hard to attain the degree of success that she was now enjoying—and she was determined to make the most of it.

★ 6 ★

"It's My Turn"

Linda Gray appeared in two different made-for-TV movies in 1980, and both roles took her in new directions as an actress. The first, "Haywire," was the prestigious screen adaptation of Brooke Hayward's best-selling book of the same name. It is the story of a prominent Hollywood family, and their descent from glamour and grandeur into mental breakdown and tragedy.

The book was a biography of actress Margaret Sullavan and her husband, celebrity agent Leland Hayward, written by their daughter, Brooke. The film put Linda in fine company, with Lee Remick as Sullavan, and Jason Robards in the part of Hayward. Prior to Sullavan's New Year's Day 1960 suicide, Hayward remarried. In the movie version, Linda played the role of the next Mrs. Hayward.

In her following movie outing that year, Linda found herself starring for the first time as the female lead. The film was called "The Wild and the Free." Gray's co-stars included actor Granville Van Dusen and several trained chimpanzees. The story centers around the first chimpanzees to be taught the same sign language used by the deaf. Linda's character in the film is patterned after famed primate expert Jane Goodall.

As conscientious scientist Miss Linda Davenport, Linda plays a naturalist who studies primate behavior. She lives in the jungles of Africa, observing a particular group of chimpanzees. Her work encompasses a life study of the chimps' societal structure and survival tactics. As college researcher Douglas Raphaelson, Van Dusen plays a behavioral scientist with the opposite line of thinking. He has a group of chimps that he is raising as human children—dressing them in clothes and teaching them sign language.

When Raphaelson's chimps are earmarked as the subjects of a college cancer research experiment, he turns to the famed Miss Davenport for help. The real conflicts start when Raphaelson arrives at Miss Davenport's camp in the jungle with his chimpanzees dressed as children. The two scientists begin arguing about the question of which society is more advanced: the human beings or the chimpanzees?

According to Linda, "I was told that to get the chimp's approval, I had to get him to offer me food and eat it the way he did. The chimp sat with his finger holding my mouth open to watch me chew. I hope I never see another banana!"

The movie "The Wild and the Free" was broadcast on November 26 and on December 23, 1980 Linda was seen on the variety special "Mac Davis—I'll Be Home For Christmas." Singing Christmas carols with Davis, the show marked Gray's musical debut on television. Other guests on the show included Melissa Manchester and Mills Watson.

Before she started filming episodes for the new "Dallas" season, Linda went to Australia to appear on that continent's annual television awards ceremony. By this point the most asked question of the summer of 1980 was, of course, "Who shot J.R.?" Recalls Linda, "I went to Australia as a presenter at their Logie Awards. On the way back we stopped in Fiji. My daughter and I were out in the surf, and I turned around, and there were five women swimming frantically toward me yelling, 'Sue Ellen, Sue Ellen! Did you shoot J.R.?' It broke me up!"

The answer to that famous question remained a mystery right up until the end. At one point during the show's annual hiatus, Gray phoned the producers to find out if she shot J.R. According to her, their answer was, "We wouldn't tell you even if you did." She simply shrugged, "I guess I'll just have to stay tuned like everyone else!"

Before any work could be done on "Dallas" that season, several of the actor's contracts had to be renewed. By early June a settlement had been reached with Patrick Duffy. However, by mid-month Larry Hagman and Linda Gray were still holding out for raises. Hagman publicly stated, "I want what's coming to me and that's that. I think it's only fair that I be properly compensated for my work on the show." Settlements were finally reached: Linda would reportly be paid $50,000 per episode; Larry would reap twice that figure.

Further complications arose that year when the Screen Actors Guild staged a strike, bringing all television production to a screeching halt. This caused the premiere of the 1980–1981 "Dallas" season to be pushed back a full seven weeks, delaying even further the resolution of the "Who shot J.R.?" puzzle.

According to Linda, when the SAG/AFTRA strike occurred, the cast had been filming pieces of ten different episodes of the show. To keep even the cast from figuring out "who shot J.R.," several reaction shots were filmed without the actors knowing who or what they were reacting to. "We'd be handed pieces of blank script for certain scenes. One day producer/director Leonard Katzman whispered to me on the set, 'Give an evil look over there—just look evil!' 'At whom?' I asked. 'I don't even know what the evil look is for!'"

Finally, on November 21, the episode entitled "No More Mr. Nice Guy" aired. However there were several twists in the plot, causing the actual murderer not to be apprehended until two episodes later. That first episode was viewed by an estimated 350 million people in 57 different countries. Advertising time on that particular show skyrocketed to the highest price ever asked on a television series: $500,000 per minute!

As it turned out, Sue Ellen was the prime suspect in the minds of several people. According to Linda Gray, she was surprised: "The idea that people think good old Sue Ellen would ever do such a thing is painful. Why, she loves J.R.—or why else would she still be at the South Fork Ranch?"

However, when the much talked about season began, the multitudes saw "good old Sue Ellen" being hauled off to jail for "attempted murder." Naturally, in good soap opera tradition, the case was hardly a cut-and-dried affair.

In the episode "No More Mr. Nice Guy," the cleaning woman at Ewing Oil discovers J.R.'s bleeding body on the floor. When he is rushed to the hospital, the Ewing clan rallys around his bedside to see if he is going to survive. Sue Ellen, however, is nowhere to be found. When we catch the first glimpse of Sue Ellen, she is coming to in her car. She had gotten so drunk the night before that she hasn't the foggiest idea how she got here. When she discovers that J.R. has been shot she hasn't a clue as to whether or not she attempted to murder her husband or not. In an emergency transfer of power, Bobby takes over Ewing Oil.

The next week's episode, entitled "Nightmare," finds J.R. regaining consciousness, and he's fighting mad when he discovers that his younger brother is running the family business. Guilt-ridden about the fateful night of the shooting, Sue Ellen showers J.R. with attention, only to have him coldly reject her sympathy. The gun that was used to shoot J.R., missing up until this time, is found by Jock at South Fork— stashed in one of J.R.'s boots. The pistol is turned over to the police, and they discover Sue Ellen's fingerprints all over it.

It is in the third episode of the season, aptly entitled "Who Done It," that the whole gory truth is unraveled. Sue Ellen is arrested and booked for attempting to murder her husband, with bail set at $100,000. That scene had one of Linda Gray's most memorable shots on the show that season: there she stands in a jail cell, wearing a chic black-and-white designer outfit, with a Dallas Police Department tag dangling from her neck, identifying her as convict number 6306.

Although the Ewings refuse to post her bail, someone mysteriously does. Sue Ellen hightails it to the only man who can help her—her shrink, Dr. Elby (actor Jeff Cooper). He hypnotizes her in an attempt to help her retrace her footsteps on the night that she blacked out, and J.R. was shot.

In a hypnotic trance, Sue Ellen remembers that although she had a gun in her possession earlier that evening, she changed purses during the course of the night, leaving herself weaponless. She had been drinking at her sister Kristin's apartment, she recalls. Then it hits her: not only did she not shoot J.R.—but her sister Kristin (actress Mary Crosby) is trying to frame her for the crime.

When she confronts J.R. and Kristin, her sister admits to having shot J.R., and also reveals that she is pregnant with his child. Guilty Kristin blackmails J.R. into dropping all of the charges against her, if he refuses, she'll publish her sordid memoirs, thus creating an even juicier scandal. Kristin ultimately agrees to leave town, and Sue Ellen's name is cleared.

Later in the season, Linda Gray's next major plotlines come from her extramarital affairs. First of all there is her flirtation with Clint Ogden (actor Monte Markham). He is an old friend of hers, and her attraction is to him is rekindled at the wedding of Lucy Ewing.

Lucy is marrying a struggling medical student named Mitch Cooper (actor Mitch McCloskey), and her wedding at the South Fork Ranch becomes the scene of several romantic liasons. Not only is Sue Ellen reintroduced to Clint, but J.R. begins to have an affair with Mitch's sister Afton (actress Audrey Landers) as well.

Meanwhile, two of the show's main characters, Ray and Pam, struggle to find out the identities of their natural parents. Through plot turns over several episodes, Ray discovers that he is actually Jock Ewing's illegitimate son, and therefore a half-brother of J.R. and Bobby. And, through her own searching, Pam locates her mother, the never-wed Rebecca Wentworth (actress Priscilla Pointer).

At one point, Sue Ellen is convinced that she is being followed. Who could possibly want to have her spied on—except J.R.? When she confronts him, he tells her that she is a "raving neurotic," suffering from a vivid imagination. Sue Ellen in turn hires her own investigator, and finds out that someone has indeed been having her trailed. But she is shocked when she finds out the identity of the man who hired the investigator: it was Dusty Farlow!

Although he was presumed dead, Dusty is very much alive and living in seclusion. As it turns out, he wanted to know Sue Ellen's whereabouts but didn't want her to find out that he was left crippled and impotent by the airplane accident. Sue Ellen confronts him and proclaims that these facts are irrelevent, because it is Dusty she really loves—not J.R.

Other plot developments that season included Ray Krebbs marrying Donna Culver, Miss Ellie seeking to divorce Jock, and J.R. and Bobby fighting over control of Ewing Oil. Sue Ellen eventually decides to end her affair with Clint, Pam finds out that she'll never have children, and nasty Kristin returns to Dallas with blackmail on her mind.

Kristin shows up to bilk child support money out of J.R. and also turns to oilman Jordan Lee (actor Don Starr), claiming that her child is his. It turns out that she is collecting checks from every man in town she ever slept with. When J.R.'s publicist, Leslie Stewart (actress Susan Flannery), reveals that she has taped evidence against J.R. regarding his dirty Asian oil deal, she, too, begins to blackmail him. And to top it off, Sue Ellen, disgusted with J.R., announces that she is leaving him and South Fork. She threatens to leave the ranch with John Ross III, but in her attempt to take the child with her, she is thrown off of the premises without her child. She leaves, hurling threats and accusations at J.R. These plot developments leave J.R. with a desire to kill all three women.

At the end of the final episode of the season, a body is discovered in the South Fork swimming pool, floating face down. It is a woman's body—but whose is it: Kristin's? Leslie's? or Sue Ellen's?

In 1981 Linda did not participate in any made-for-TV movies, but she did film a two-part daytime television special about human sexuality entitled, "The Body Human." The first part was called "The Loving Process—Women"; the second was its male counterpart, "The Loving Process—Men." They were broadcast on November 3 and 4, and again on November 10 and 11. The show's message was that it was time to put aside religious taboos and talk in an honest fashion about the mechanics of human sexuality. Both programs dealt with the topic of sexuality in a straightforward and candid fashion.

Linda, who had just celebrated her forty-first birthday when the programs were broadcast, made several frank statements about her own sexual feelings and observations about sex after forty. According to her, "Sex does not get better as you get older, but it can be more meaningful and comfortable. I think sex becomes more romantic after forty. I certainly haven't lost any interest in sex, that's for sure.

"You have to work at making yourself look good, because that tells your partner what you think of him. You can't let yourself grow stale, because if you do, so will your marriage. You've got to be imaginative and keep looking for ways to keep the spark in your romance. Turning forty was no problem for me. I really keep myself together. I exercise a lot, I don't drink. I know I sound like a drill sergeant, but that's the way I am. I have a lady friend who visits me every day at lunch and works out with me. I use barbells and weights and keep nothing more than a salad in my refrigerator. I also run and ride horseback. I learned a long time ago that those are all things that make you a vital person."

Talking about the sexual mores that she was raised with, Linda explained, "When I grew up, sex was a common taboo. I was taught sex was a dirty thing, but I'm teaching my daughter that sex is a warm, tender, loving thing. But I also tell her sex should be special. If you give sex away without love, it's not worth anything. I want her to use her own mind and judgment. I want her to know exactly what machinery is there and how it works. And you don't fool around with it. If you do, you pay the price and have to be responsible for it. I freely advise my daughter to be her own person. I don't want her to grow up thinking the same things I did. I can't put down my parents—they did what they thought was right. I have to be honest with her. I want her to know all aspects of her sexuality and be prepared for whatever comes along."

Discussing "The Body Human," Linda said, "I know the 'Moral Majority' is out to get me for the way I think and the character I play on 'Dallas.' They'll think the show I did is dirty. But, I don't care because

I know I've done something positive, and they're doing something negative."

One of the topics that Linda spoke about on the show was faked orgasms. She asked, "Why can't we be able to say, 'I don't want to fake anymore. I love you. I want you to share all of my experiences. I want to be encompassed by the whole of you, touch you, hold you, share you with me.' It's not fair to fake an orgasm in a relationship. When I was first married, I was afraid to challenge my husband, to say 'I don't like this.' I worried that maybe he wouldn't love me anymore. Now if I'm turned on by his kissing my neck, I'm going to say so."

Sex also played a large role in the continuing saga of "Dallas." The 1981–1982 season of the show presented some new challenges for the producers. First and foremost on the minds of everyone was how to deal with a real-life tragedy. Actor Jim Davis, who had played Jock, the paternal stronghold of the Ewing family, had died earlier in the year. Instead of replacing Davis with another actor, it was decided to build an elaborate plot twist, leading up to the death of Jock Ewing. Ultimately, the writers had Jock doing business in South America. In a freak accident involving a helicopter that he was riding in, Jock plummeted to his death. But the final acceptance of Jock's demise didn't come until the fourteenth episode, well into the season.

Meanwhile, in the opening episode Cliff Barnes has an appointment at South Fork to discuss some oil business with Bobby. While he waits for Bobby, he wanders out to the pool and sees the body that was shown in the previous season's "cliffhanger" episode.

He dives into the swimming pool in an effort to save whomever it is.

By this point in the show's history, the solution to any of the previous season's cliffhangers had become such a guarded secret that even the actors were not allowed to find out what was going to happen on the show. In an effort to ensure secrecy, three different swimming pool scenes were filmed before the season hiatus began. Linda Gray, Victoria Principal, and Mary Crosby each had to film the same scene once so that even they didn't know who the real victim would be.

Ultimately, it turned out to be Kristin who was floating lifelessly in the Ewing pool. Since it was Cliff who discovered the body, J.R. tries to frame him for Kristin's murder. However, it was J.R. who had the strongest motive, and he is arrested for the murder. But an autopsy reveals such a high concentration of barbiturates in Kristin's bloodstream that it is obvious that she fell into the pool on her own. J.R. is released from custody, only to find out that he has even more to worry about at South Fork.

First of all, Sue Ellen is divorcing him. And second, Pam has kidnapped little John Ross III in a fit of maternal justice, and delivered him to Sue Ellen, who is now living with Dusty and his father, Clayton Farlow (actor Howard Keel), at their ranch, The Southern Cross.

By the third episode of the season, J.R. hatches a plan to have Miss Ellie go to The Southern Cross to visit John Ross and to seize him. Miss Ellie is flown in by helicopter to kidnap her grandson, but she decides at the last minute that she can't go through it. In the next episode, J.R. and Sue Ellen are in court, arguing for custody of their son. Although J.R. sets out to prove that his wife is living in sin, Dusty's doctors submit signed affidavits to prove that he isn't even capable of having sex. Sue Ellen wins round one of the battle, and she and her son continue to reside at The Southern Cross with Dusty and Clayton.

Over the next several episodes, the death of Jock is the central focus of the show. In the meantime, Pam is still despondent over her inability to have a child, and suffers a nervous breakdown. Without Pam's knowledge, Bobby arranges for them to adopt Kristin's orphaned baby boy. They name him Christopher, and although Pam does not know the identity of the boy's natural mother, having her own baby helps her snap out of her suicidal depression.

For several episodes, the three Ewing boys—J.R., Bobby, and Ray—all fight over the money and property left behind after Jock's death. Amid all these struggles, J.R. and Cliff each discover that they still love Sue Ellen, and she finds herself the prize in their battle for her attentions.

J.R. sets a business trap for Cliff, and Cliff falls for it. Before long Sue Ellen discovers that J.R. only wants her so he can have his son back at South Fork. And, after Cliff has blown all his money on J.R.'s bogus scheme, he asks Sue Ellen for a four-million-dollar loan. She realizes then that he only wants her for her money.

Cliff's only ally is his new girlfriend, Afton, and J.R. has by now enlisted his latest partner in crime, Pam and Cliff's estranged, long-lost sister, Katherine Wentworth (actress Morgan Brittany). When it comes time to vote the new president of Ewing Oil into office, J.R. blackmails Bobby. If Bobby doesn't vote for J.R., J.R.

will inform Pam that the baby they've just adopted is in fact Kristin and J.R.'s child. Rather than cave in to J.R.'s threats, Bobby tells Pam that Christopher may in fact be J.R.'s child. She is devastated, but she forgives Bobby.

Somehow, in her own masochistic and mysterious way, Sue Ellen again falls for J.R.'s charms, and agrees to remarry him. After a trip to California to examine the birth records, Pam and Bobby discover that Kristin miscarried that particular baby, and that Christopher is no relation to J.R.—much to their relief.

This season's cliffhanger involves Cliff Barnes. Despondent over losing Sue Ellen and his business, and overcome with the feeling that he is a complete failure, Cliff attempts suicide. As the season ends, the question is: Will Cliff live?

In 1982 Linda Gray filmed another made-for-TV movie. This time around she was the star of a drama about a divorcing woman, centering on how she takes control of her new life as once again single. Entitled "Not in Front of the Children," the film co-starred John Getz and John Lithgow. In the film, Linda's character has a younger boyfriend move in with her and then finds herself in a fight for the custody of her children.

According to Linda, "By now I think people know Sue Ellen isn't Linda Gray, but I still think it's important to break out every now and then and remind them I can do something else. That's why I did 'The Wild and the Free,' 'Haywire,' and last year, 'The Body Human,' plus this film. It's about whether a woman with two children should live with a man.

"After I agreed to do it," she explained, "the script was totally rewritten to personalize it for me. I had a lot of input. There were things about the original script I didn't like. She had no family or friends. It was like playing Sue Ellen again. We gave her friends and made her life fuller. I definitely look for roles that are different from Sue Ellen. I always had visions of what I want to do. They're not what I'm offered. I get offers to play the wife of powerful men. In this film I didn't want to be rich and I didn't want to be neurotic. I wanted a woman's film that would show a stronger woman than Sue Ellen.

"I like the controversy," said Linda with regard to the film. "After all, Bette Davis never concerned herself about that when she accepted a role. In 'Not in Front of the Children' I play Nancy Carruthers, a divorced woman with two daughters who is in love with a younger man, Dr. Paul Adams [actor John Getz]. While he's willing to marry, my character feels strongly that she should be able to live her own life and not be pressured for hypocritical moral reasons. She's not ready for a commitment. She wants to be her own person. But the home situation is a close, loving one and the daughters are happy, which is in contrast to her previous situation.

"Some people will object to the idea. But the times are such that this is something many divorced women are facing. It's a fact that's going on right now—a woman falls in love with a man, but she doesn't want to get married yet. So he moves in. How do you explain it to the children? That's the children's dilemma: 'Do we have two daddies?' 'What do we call him?' 'Is he going to sleep with you?' People are no longer accepting the dictates of what society thinks should be done, but following their own feelings in the matter."

Since divorce, child custody, and independence

were so strongly fixed in Linda's mind at this time, how was her real-life marriage going? According to her, her relationship with Ed Thrasher was quite sound throughout 1982. However, other sources began to report that this wasn't quite the case.

Ed had long since left Capitol Records and moved on to Warner Brothers Records. After that he formed his own design company, Ed Thrasher & Associates. In 1981 he completed one of his most impressive and highly visible projects ever: the cover art for the Grammy Award-winning Lena Horne album, "The Lady And Her Music."

When asked about her relationship with Ed, Linda explained at the time, "He's really a special man. For a marriage to survive now with all the pulls and pressures is difficult. But we've had open communication and been able to discuss what's going on. People always say you have to work at marriage. I think a good relationship should just happen—out of respect, appreciation for each other's uniqueness and exciting times."

However, she also admitted, "During our years together, both Ed and I have changed. We've grown together. We have a great life. I've got the career I've always wanted, and now Ed has his own business doing promotion for movies. But we've had our rocky periods—maybe not as earth-shattering as Sue Ellen's and J.R.'s, but traumatic all the same."

Stormier times were definitely ahead for the couple. Ed was beginning to resent Linda's passion for her work, and he felt that he'd rather see her playing the happy housewife role with equal zest. But it was not destined to work out that way.

However, for the time being, the biggest and most

controversial change that Linda would make before starting the 1982–1983 "Dallas" season revolved around her hairstyle. The producers of the show literally freaked out when she showed up for work with her trademark long tresses cut off.

"I did my own personal survey," she explained, "looking at everyone on TV, and I thought all the leading ladies were quite alike. I just wanted to look different. I thought I needed a change. And throughout history, when women have decided to change their look, the first thing they've gone for is the hair. I had had it with long hair. I don't like to be a carbon copy of everybody else. Also, I knew that short hair was coming back in style, and I didn't want to be a follower of that trend. I wanted to be one of the leaders."

Her new look was so radically different that when she flew into New York City before the new "Dallas" season began airing, she was almost totally unrecognized by fans. In fact, she breezed into several Broadway shows incognito, including *Agnes Of God*, *Dreamgirls*, and a preview performance of *Cats*. Instead of mobbing her for autographs, people must have surmised, 'That can't be Linda Gray—her hair's so short!'

In the last glimpse of Linda that "Dallas" viewers had at the end of the previous season, Sue Ellen was standing by the bedside of Cliff Barnes, praying that he would come out of his coma. "When the season ended," Linda explained, "I was wearing a sweater, pants, and had long hair. We did a direct cut from that to start the new season. There I was in the same sweater and pants—and my hair is suddenly short. I rationalize it this way: I'm in the hospital and distraught. So, being a typical socialite, I go out while

Cliff's in a coma and have my hair cut. There I am with this whole new look. It's hysterical! But it was also something I needed to do.

"Frankly, the producers weren't too happy," she admitted. In fact, they tried to talk her into wearing a hairpiece so that she would look like she did in the last scene from the previous season, but she flatly refused.

Naturally, the most dramatic thing to happen to Sue Ellen during the 1982–1983 season on the show was her remarriage to J.R. In the middle of the previous season, overwhelmed by everything that was going on, Sue Ellen had moved off the Southern Cross Ranch and into her own town house to sort things out.

Discussing the new season, Linda precluded it by explaining, "The writers took me away from the ranch and put me in my little town house, and then realized that a key element of the show was Larry's relationship with me. I think they are trying to find a way to bring me back to South Fork. There is no question that my favorite scenes in the show are when Larry and I are together. There is this fabulous creative stimulation that happens between the two of us that is really quite magical. It has always been like that.

"The thing I find fascinating is going into a scene which is just a 'throwaway,' and poorly written, and thinking, 'What am I going to do with this?' By the time we're through, we've turned it from dull to dynamite. Larry is a very creative and stimulating actor. And he is a very giving actor. We love spontaneity in our scenes. We ad-lib a bit and get some juices going. Even the love scenes are fun, and we adore the fight scenes."

However, Linda was getting a little mad at the character she was playing on the show. She was finding new strength and growth in her own personal life; why couldn't Sue Ellen grow a bit more too? According to her at the time, "I get so angry at Sue Ellen. She's so dumb. I wish she were more intelligent. I had really hoped last season after she divorced J.R. that she would show a little strength. She was married to this man, she knows all his conniving ways, but she still falls for his line. She loves him and I think because of that, blindly believes him—which is devastating to me as a person."

The 1982–1983 "Dallas" season opens with a guilt-ridden Sue Ellen blaming herself for Cliff's attempted suicide. She is so convinced of her responsibility for what happened that she tells J.R. that if Cliff dies, she won't remarry. In the second episode of the season, entitled "Where There's A Will," Cliff comes out of his coma, and J.R. convinces Sue Ellen that he actually does love her, and wants to marry her again. Of course Sue Ellen does not realize that a large part of his motivation for wanting her back is the fact that his young son is also a shareholder in Ewing Oil, and the battle for control is officially on.

In an emergency meeting of the Ewings, J.R. is voted out of his post as president of Ewing Oil. J.R. turns to the pursuit of Holly Harwood (actress Lois Chiles) for a controlling interest in her own oil company. In the fourth episode of the season, Sue Ellen is still contemplating whether or not she'll accept J.R.'s proposal. Taking a trip down to the Southern Cross, she nearly flips when she finds out that Dusty has married. Although Sue Ellen was the one who had helped him regain the ability to walk again, it seems that, in her absence, another woman has helped him regain his ability to have sex. She is eventually persuaded to remarry J.R. By the time of the wedding, Jock's will has been read, and its terms pit Bobby and J.R. against each other for the control of Ewing Oil.

The sequence in which Sue Ellen and J.R. remarry actually spanned two episodes of the show. For the wedding, Linda Gray was clad in a chic light-gray silk suit, carried a bouquet of coral pink roses, and wore a 13.5 carat diamond wedding ring. Naturally, the wedding ceremony erupts into a battle before it is over, with J.R. and Cliff engaged in a fist fight in their tuxedos.

In other developments on the show that season, Bobby and Pam's marriage hits the rocks, and Pam meets and falls in love with handsome Mark Graison (actor John Beck). Miss Ellie comes out of mourning and begins seeing Clayton Farlow. Soon after his wedding to Sue Ellen, J.R. begins to romance Holly Harwood. And Lucy falls in love with Ray's nephew, Mickey Trotter (actor Timothy Patrick Murphy).

While trying to thwart J.R. in one of his business deals, Cliff is unable to attend an important meeting, so his mother, Rebecca Wentworth, boards a private plane to attend the meeting in his place. The plane crashes, and Cliff and Pam's sister, Katherine, vows to get even with them for their mother's death.

Later in the season, Holly Harwood realizes that she is being used by J.R., and she decides to get even by arranging for Sue Ellen to catch them together in Holly's bed. When Sue Ellen finds them she realizes that J.R. has remarried her only to get John Ross III back at South Fork, and she returns to her oldest and dearest friend: the liquor bottle.

As the fifth season winds down to a close, Sue Ellen

jumps into J.R.'s car to run away from him, and Mickey gets into the car as well to try to stop her from hurting herself. Another car sideswipes them, and their car flips over into a ditch. Sue Ellen escapes with minor injuries, but Mickey is paralyzed for life. Everyone blames Sue Ellen, but what they don't realize is that the accident was a set up intended for J.R., payment for one of his underhanded business deals.

In the final episode of the season, entitled "Ewing Inferno," Ray shows up at South Fork seeking revenge. Everyone gets wise to the accident, and Ray is determined to make J.R. pay for ruining his nephew's life. During the ensuing fistfight, a lighted candle is knocked over igniting a batch of flammable painting supplies. Soon the main house at South Fork is in flames with J.R., Ray, Sue Ellen, and John Ross in it. Who will survive?

Meanwhile, Linda Gray's own life off camera had begun to seem a bit like a soap opera as well. In March of 1983 the news became official: Linda Gray had moved out of the ranch house that she had shared with Ed Thrasher for the past twelve years, and she had taken up residence in a beach house in Malibu. After twenty years as husband and wife, their marriage was over, and Linda was living on her own.

After "Dallas" became a huge success, Linda juggled the roles of wife and mother with her full-time acting career. In this 1979 photo Gray rides a three-wheeler with her son Jeff while a trio of neighborhood kids join in on the fun. *(AP/Wide World)*

With her ex-husband Ed Thrasher and her children Jeff and Kehly, Linda enjoys a social outing in the early 1980s. Ed was opposed to Linda's acting career. *(Star File)*

Linda enjoys a private moment with her daughter Kehly in 1979. *(AP/Wide World)*

The original cast of "Dallas" (left to right): Larry Hagman, Linda Gray, Jim Davis, Barbara Bel Geddes (seated), Patrick Duffy, Charlene Tilton (foreground), Victoria Principal, and Steve Kanaly. The show premiered in 1978, and has been a hit ever since. *(AP/Wide World)*

"Who shot J.R.?" was the most-asked question of 1980. Larry Hagman as the dastardly J.R. Ewing was wheelchair bound for several segments of the show while the facts behind the mysterious shooting were unraveled. Two of the prime suspects were Steve Kanaly as Ray Krebbs (left) and Linda Gray as Sue Ellen (right). *(AP/Wide World)*

Linda Gray behind bars! When the "Who shot J.R.?" episode of "Dallas" was aired on November 21, 1980, a record number of viewers tuned in— estimated at 350 million people in fifty-seven different countries. *(AP/Wide World)*

Linda's greatest admirer on the "Dallas" set has been her co-star Larry Hagman. He proclaims of Gray, "She has proven she can play anything: a psychotic, an alcoholic, the rejected woman, the woman on the edge of promiscuity, the woman having problems with her mother and sister, the woman who deals with the infatuation of a boy less than half her age." *(AP/Wide World)*

"I think Sue Ellen is the most fascinating woman on TV today," says Linda. "Every time I read a new script, I'm amazed at what she has to go through." Here a distraught Sue Ellen carries her son John Ross III (actor Omri Katz) in her arms. *(AP/Wide World)*

During the seventh season of "Dallas," Linda Gray and Victoria Principal filmed several on-location scenes in Hong Kong. The two actresses are discussing a scene with the episode's director, Leonard Katzman. *(AP/Wide World)*

Linda and two of her co-stars of the 1980 made-for-TV movie "The Wild and the Free." In the film she played a behavioral scientist studying chimpanzees. *(AP/Wide World)*

Linda Gray made headlines in 1983 when she divorced Ed Thrasher, her husband of twenty-one years. He resented her success on "Dallas." "I couldn't stop working just because I was a wife and mother," she explains. *(David Loar/Retna Ltd.)*

After her divorce, Linda began a three-year affair with trumpet player Paul Constanza, who she claims was "everything my husband was not." *(Vinnie Zuffante/Star File)*

Linda claims that her own personality is totally different from emotionally unstable Sue Ellen Ewing. In private, Gray relishes the opportunity to hang up the designer clothes and put on a comfortable pair of blue jeans. *(AP/Wide World)*

Author Mark Bego, Linda Gray, and fashion designer to the stars, Bob Mackie, at the opening of Diana Vreeland's costume exhibit at the Metropolitan Museum in New York City, December 1983. *(Roger Glazer)*

Clothes-conscious Linda Gray flew to Paris in March of 1984 to view the newest fashions. Here she is seen chatting with designer Yves St. Laurent. *(AP/Wide World)*

Today, absorbed in her work as a TV star and director, Linda is finally able to control her own career and personal life. *(AP/Wide World)*

Linda and her son Jeff arrive for the December 1985 premiere of *Out of Africa*. Jeff is fascinated with cinematography, and has worked behind the scenes on the set of "Dallas." *(AP/Wide World)*

Gray and her daughter Kehly have a close relationship. According to Linda, "My kids have not known an 'Ozzie and Harriet' kind of life. They have seen a real human mommy working and struggling." *(Barry King/Star File)*

"Being sexy has nothing to do with the outside of a woman," proclaims Linda. "Women who have the most sex appeal are those who enjoy life, who take pleasure in themselves, and who live according to their own rules—and not those imposed by others!" *(Walter McBride/Retna Ltd.)*

Linda carefully studies a camera angle, amid her directorial debut in 1986. For Gray, becoming a director on "Dallas" represented the fulfillment of a lifelong dream. *(AP/Wide World)*

Linda Gray is living proof that the glamorous life can continue after forty! *(Greg Gorman/Gamma Liaison)*

★ 7 ★

Alone Again and Loving It

Linda had known for several months that the situation between herself and Ed was heading toward an irreconcilable end. She wanted to keep moving and growing in her life, and Ed was not interested in changing. He wanted her to increase her duties as wife and mother; he even implored her to quit her acting career on "Dallas."

For a long time Linda didn't seriously consider divorce as an acceptable alternative to the pressures she was experiencing in her personal life. Her children, and her own real-life role as "mother," kept her from making any rash decisions.

"There are enormous difficulties in balancing priorities," Linda explained before she made the decision to leave Ed. By this point, her son Jeff was eighteen, and her daughter Kehly was sixteen. "Everyone pulls. Sure, my children are grown, but I still have enormous guilt because a part of me feels I should be home more than I am. And maybe I *should* be. How do I know they won't go looking for me in negative ways? In other words, how do I know they won't get into drugs, sex, or some kind of other trouble just to get my undivided attention? That bothers me. I do everything I know how to do, and pray to God that it's good enough. But, before all else, I must work; I must be my own person. If I please me, then I can please others. Loving yourself makes you more loving to and of and for others."

One of the ways in which Linda played both actress and mother was through the trips that she would take with Jeff and Kehly when she had to do location work in Dallas. Since Jeff was interested in learning about cinematography, Linda got him a job on the set. She wanted him to understand that show business is first and foremost a business.

"Well, I'm not sure there's ever a perfect time for fame," Linda contemplated. "If it'd happened to me when my children were babies—I just don't know. They're pretty unaffected by it now, especially since theirs is a rural school with no show-business people. The only time they got any special attention was with the 'Who shot J.R.?' mystery. Oh, I suppose my daughter likes the glamour of openings and parties and that sort of thing. But my son has worked with me behind the scenes on the show, and he realizes it's not all limos and pretty clothes. He really understands the exhaustion and tedium that go along with it. They both do. And, I believe they're both proud of me.

"I'm really tired of being picked on vis-à-vis my kids," said Linda of her working mother life-style. "Yes, I've always worked—even during my pregnancies—and it was tough to get it all done. Often, when I didn't have a summer vacation, we'd use Easter time as our 'family vacation.' But where do people get the idea that actresses and actors are unfit parents? I know women doctors and lawyers who spend less time with their children than I. And you can be a terrible mother if you're home twenty-four hours a day. A lot of people insist you can't have a career and kids, yet you can. It's not easy, but then, most of life isn't."

It was while she was filming the 1982–1983 season of "Dallas" that Ed began to pressure her to quit her acting career and resign as Sue Ellen. According to Linda, she had no intention of doing any such thing. "I needed to work to be fulfilled as a person," she explained. "I couldn't and wouldn't, simply stop just because someone urged me to quit—even if it was my husband. While Ed at first said he was happy that I was doing what I wanted to do, he was also fearful: what would my career do to my family? He wanted me to quit, but I couldn't stop working just because I was a wife and mother. I flatly refused to give it up."

During this period, while Linda was deciding whether or not to leave Ed, Larry Hagman and his wife Maj (pronounced 'My') were her most supportive friends. Although Larry plays the dastardly J.R. on "Dallas," he really came to her rescue as only a warm and sincere friend would do.

Linda made the decision that she would leave the house where she and Ed and the children had lived in Canyon Country. She moved into a rented house in Malibu. All of this was done without a word said to the press. However, it wasn't long before the news leaked out, and several erroneous rumors were published about the break up of her marriage.

It seems that the landlady who rented her the Malibu house phoned her sister in Germany. The landlady's sister happened to talk to a journalist over there about Linda Gray and Larry Hagman renting a house in Malibu. Soon the story had been blown totally out of proportion. Hagman had recommended the house to Linda, but when the item appeared in the German papers, the implication was that Linda and Larry had leased a love nest and that Linda had left her husband for Larry. Linda was very embarrassed by all of the rumors, claiming that it especially hurt her family. "They hate all of this," she exclaimed. "It's humiliating to us all."

At any rate, the news was out, and the break up of Linda Gray and Ed Thrasher became one of the year's hottest Hollywood divorces. Once the matter was no longer a secret, Linda settled down to the task of learning to live alone once again. Both Jeff and Kehly were free to shuttle back and forth between the ranch house in Canyon Country and their mother's new Malibu beach home. Linda was able to adjust to her new solo status quickly. For the first time in over twenty years she was alone again and loving it.

She explained at the time that her adjustment period was made much easier by her friends. "Larry and Maj have practically adopted me as their daughter," she laughed. "After the divorce they took me on trips to Europe with them, they found the house in Malibu for me so I wouldn't be alone, and they even played Welcome Wagon lady for me by greeting me in the house with balloons, champagne, and a machine which filled the building with bubbles. Larry and Maj can do some crazy things, but so can I in my friendship with them."

One of Linda's first solo evenings on the town was in March of 1983. She attended a taping of the television special "Motown 25" by herself and admits that it was very bizarre for her at first. "I was still living in the rented beach house," she recalls, "and I had booked a limo to take me to the Pasadena Civic Center for Motown's anniversary celebration. My publicist, Richard Grant, was to meet me there. It had never crossed my mind to invite a man to escort me until the car pulled up and I saw all this hoopla—red carpet, paparazzi, klieg lights. When the attendants opened both doors of the limo, my heart sank. 'Please shut the other door,' I said. 'There's no one on that side. I'm here alone tonight.' Then I walked in with my head up high, thinking, 'If *this* isn't the test, I don't know what is!'"

The legal arrangements of Linda and Ed's split-up were settled rather quickly and quietly. She left the Canyon Country house on February 19, 1983, and filed the official separation papers on March 4 in Los Angeles Superior Court. The actual divorce papers were filed by Gray in early June, and the couple agreed on joint custody of their two children. By the end of the year, it was all over.

One of the things that Linda worried about the most was her children's reaction to the divorce. Would they blame her for dissolving the family atmosphere they had grown up in? According to Linda, the effect was quite the opposite. "We grew closer," she claims, "because they saw me go through tremendous hurts and disappointments. It was incredible what my children saw. They saw me cry. They saw me hurt. They saw men come calling who didn't care about me, but who wanted to date me because I'm a celebrity. They saw me sitting home alone on Saturday nights. They thought, 'This is a Hollywood sex symbol? This person on the couch with the dog?'

"My kids have not known an 'Ozzie and Harriet' kind of life. They have seen a real human mommy, working and struggling. They saw that and gave me love and respect. Maybe the relationship between the three of us wouldn't be this strong if I had stayed married and unhappy," she says in retrospect.

By late summer, Linda was feeling more confident about her divorce decision. "My son, Jeff, is nineteen and in college this fall," she explained at the time. "My daughter, Kehly, is seventeen and in her last year of high school. They still need me, but they are their own people now. They are becoming self-sufficient. I sort of like being alone, being able to pamper myself. I used to try so hard to be one of the gang. If someone said, 'Let's go here and do this,' I would always be out the door, ready to go, never considering that my body was so tired I could hardly move. Now I rest when I'm tired."

For Linda the decision to divorce eventually resulted in a great deal of self-discovery, and a newfound freedom from guilt. "I used to feel guilty taking the time to get a massage or a facial," she says of her old way of thinking. "Now I realize that I owe it to myself to take care of those things. We all need to take the time. We feel better, and it's good for us to look as good as we can. Not just because I'm an actress. Because I'm a person. And, I'm not trying so hard to be Superwoman anymore. When I'm sad I cry, and when I'm angry I yell. It's just a good release. I was always so anxious about that before.''

She admitted, however, that ''it's very strange to walk into a party alone, not being part of a couple. I'm just as self-conscious as anyone else would be. But it's interesting too, to watch yourself and see how you do, see if you can handle the situation.''

It wasn't long before Linda Gray found romance. During her first couple of months back in the Hollywood whirl of premieres and parties, she was seen out with one of three main escorts. First there was her publicist Dick Grant, but that was really a business friendship. The second man she was seen dining with was Brazilian jeweler Jorge Miguel. Again, that was a business-related friendship, as Jorge was responsible for supplying the show ''Dallas'' with genuine jewelry-on-loan for film purposes. The third man she was linked with was a handsome cameraman named Craig Denault. Denault is seven years younger than Linda, and at the time had just ended an affair with actress Morgan Fairchild. Although there was a lot of speculation in the gossip columns, Denault turned out to be a long-time friend of Gray's, and nothing serious developed.

The real romance came that autumn, when Linda began seeing a trumpet player named Paul Constanza. Linda had just turned forty-three, and Constanza was thirty-two. Coincidently on the 1983–1984 ''Dallas'' season, which was airing at the time, Linda's TV character, Sue Ellen, was also having a fling with a younger man. The character Sue Ellen was involved with was her son's twenty-year-old camp counselor, Peter Richards (actor Christopher Atkins). Women who are fascinated with, and involved in, ''older woman/younger man'' relationships are said to be in throes of what might be called "the Phaedra complex."

When the filming of that storyline began, Linda was rather candid about her views on that particular subject. Little did Linda realize that her own life was about to imitate that of her TV character.

"I think it's great," said Linda, when asked about the subject. "In the U.S., we're the only society that thinks it's kind of strange. You know, they've been doing it in Europe for years. Frankly, I don't feel that age has anything to do with anything—period. I hate it when they write your name in a story and it's 'Linda Gray, ninety-seven.' Look, there are some very mature younger guys and there are some very immature older men. As long as two people have a wonderful, charismatic feeling toward each other, then why not? Age shouldn't hinder anything. If a sixty-five-year-old guy goes out with a nineteen-year-old woman, that's considered terrific, but when a woman does it, eyebrows are raised. I'm tired of all this, and it's embarrassing that this country even brings up the subject of equal rights."

According to Linda, affairs of this sort have always existed, but it has only been in the 1980s that more and more women are admitting to it. "Now that it's very fashionable, people are saying, 'to hell with the old standards, we're going to do what we want.' I feel that it's healthy, that it's great!"

From the very beginning of the Sue Ellen/Peter Richards plotline on the show that season, Gray was worried that the subject would be mishandled. She was especially concerned that the story would only be told from a very male point of view, and she wanted more control over her character.

She pointed out that on the show, "Producers, writers, everybody's a male. I told them . . . that if they were going to go ahead with the affair between me and Chris, then I wanted some more input. I wanted them to show how a woman felt. What would she do? How would she feel? What does she do about it? I wanted those feelings to come across. I wanted to give them my views so that they could incorporate them into the storyline. My request was never acknowledged, so it put me in a very awkward position, because I want to be listened to. I get to a lot of people . . . our show reaches a lot of people. I don't want it to be taken for granted that, 'Oh sure, Sue Ellen's going to hop into bed with this guy.' That cannot happen; I just can't deal with it like that."

While that season's episodes were being filmed, Linda admitted that she had a lot of apprehension. "Sue Ellen has never been too concerned about her morals anyway," she laughingly explained. "But I was concerned that *if*—and underline the 'if,' because I don't know where the love affair is going—if it does take place, then it has to be done in a way that makes me feel comfortable.

"On camera we are so comfortable with each other. He's wonderful, I just adore him [Christopher Atkins]. We had this immediate love for each other. And he's been fun to work with. Chris is willing to learn, and I think that we've both helped each other. I don't know how it's going to end up. They [the producers and writers] don't tell me anything, and that's the problem. I'm totally in the dark. I get a script three days before we shoot it and then it's, 'Oh, my God, what do I do now?' So it's the frustration of wondering what they are going to do with us, and if they do it and I don't like it—then what?"

As one might expect in a soap opera, and especially the unpredictably outrageous "Dallas," Sue Ellen and Peter not only consummate their affair, but there is also raised the traumatic question of whether or not he has gotten her pregnant. It was truly one of the spicier plotlines for the actress in her ten years of playing Sue Ellen.

Here is what ultimately transpired between Sue Ellen and Peter Richards during the program's sixth season: After Bobby and the local fire department come to the rescue, all of the inhabitants of South Fork escape the fire, and Sue Ellen makes the important discovery that, had it not been for J.R. swindling Walt Driscoll (actor Ben Piazza), the car she was driving wouldn't have been run off the road, and Mickey wouldn't have been paralyzed for life. So, in her anger, she announces that, although they have recently remarried, she and J.R. will be sleeping in separate rooms, and that their relationship should be considered an "open marriage." Realizing that the accident—and Mickey's paralysis—wasn't her fault, she swears off drinking.

Sue Ellen isn't necessarily looking for an affair when Peter Richards comes into her life. Her son, John Ross III, has become quite shy and withdrawn, presumably from having been exposed to so many family traumas at South Fork. When Peter Richards, the boy's camp counselor, shows a genuine interest in bringing him out of his shell, Sue Ellen is deeply touched. She encourages Peter to come to the ranch to help John Ross with his swimming lessons, having no idea that her son's counselor is going to fall in love with her.

Meanwhile, Ray can't stand to watch his nephew suffer in the hospital. When Mickey slips into a coma—destined to remain a vegetable for the rest of his life—Ray pulls the plug on his life support machine. Lucy is devastated by Mickey's death, and Ray is arrested for manslaughter. When the time for the annual Oil Baron's Ball comes around, Sue Ellen fixes Peter up as Lucy's escort. Nonetheless, it is made clear that it's Sue Ellen, not Lucy, that Peter is interested in.

When Peter eventually confesses his love to Sue Ellen, she decides that, although their frequent meetings have been platonic, they shouldn't see each other any more. However, since J.R. continues to emotionally abuse her, Sue Ellen soon finds herself flattered by Peter's sincere love for her.

Peter tells Sue Ellen that he is going to quit college, and he rents an apartment so that they can be discreetly alone together. Sue Ellen agrees to continue seeing him, but only if he returns to his college classes. Although Sue Ellen knows that this is an impossible situation, they ultimately consummate their love affair.

One afternoon Sue Ellen and Peter are in a restaurant and several of Peter's classmates come in. What happens next convinces her that things have gone too far: she is mistaken for his mother. With this she realizes that the whole thing is very wrong and that she must end the affair.

A couple of episodes later, Sue Ellen has a minor automobile accident, and is taken to the hospital. When J.R. shows up to take her home, the doctor takes him aside to tell him how sorry he is that Sue

Ellen has lost her baby! Baby? What baby? And for that matter, J.R. wonders, who's baby is it? Since he has only slept with Sue Ellen once in the past couple of months, he surmises that Sue Ellen has been carrying Peter's baby. Despite their marital problems and his own extramarital affairs, he isn't about to let Sue Ellen cheat on him! In a jealous rage, J.R. decides to get rid of Peter himself.

J.R. has one of his henchmen plant a bag of cocaine on Peter, and he has him arrested for drug possession. Knowing that the arrest and ensuing scandal will ruin Peter's life, he blackmails the boy: If Peter leaves Dallas immediately, he will see to it that the charges are dropped. Peter really has no choice but to agree, so he ends his relationship with Sue Ellen.

While all of this is going on, the rest of the characters have been on a marital merry-go-round as well. Pam and Bobby divorce, and Bobby starts dating his old girlfriend Jenna Wade (actress Priscilla Presley). Ray's manslaughter charges are dropped. Pam makes wedding plans with Mark Graison, and Miss Ellie agrees to marry Clayton Farlow. By the end of the season Pam discovers that Mark has an incurable illness and it appears that he has committed suicide by staging a plane crash. But, no body is found. (It was later revealed that Mark is searching the globe for a cure to his illness and wants to spare Pam the grief.) Also, a South Fork houseguest, Clayton's deranged sister Jessica Montford (actress Alexis Smith) turns out to be a murderess. After an elaborate kidnapping, Jessica almost succeeds with her plan of killing Miss Ellie before the wedding can take place. The conclusion of the sixth season finds Cliff Barnes striking the biggest oil deposit in Texas, giving him the money to overtake

J.R. in their never-ending feud. And Bobby lies bleeding on the floor of J.R.'s office, from a gunshot wound intended for J.R.

In August of 1983, while the cast and crew of "Dallas" were on location to begin filming that particular season, the show experienced its first major security problem. Linda Gray and Larry Hagman each received several death threats, and it was believed that a deranged mental patient was trying to shoot one or both of them. Certain mentally unstable persons are unable to differentiate between actors and the characters they portray on TV, and this has always been a problem for television crews. In fact, when members of the "Dallas" cast received random threats, they are routinely investigated and usually dismissed.

But in 1983 a couple of incidents occurred that were too potentially dangerous to ignore. Larry Hagman was staying in a rented house that belonged to a land developer named Henry Kyle. On July 22 Kyle was murdered in Los Angeles, and shortly thereafter, Linda Gray's Dallas hotel room was ransacked. After that, the cast was moved into high-security living quarters, and bodyguards were assigned to the sets during filming of the show. Gray and Hagman sincerely feared for their lives.

"This whole thing has gotten out of hand," said Linda about the usual accessibility strangers had to the show's sets. "As if the 108-degree temperature doesn't make things bad enough, a local radio station every hour on the hour broadcasts *exactly* where we're shooting the show. So thousands of fans show up and run riot all over the place. It's staggering. I've never seen anything like it in my life. It's really awfully frightening."

Eventually it was proven that Kyle's murder and the break-in at Linda's room at the Dallas Marriott Hotel were unreleated incidents. Following the scare, security measures were beefed up, and soon it was business as usual once more for Linda Gray and the rest of the cast of "Dallas."

On July 8, 1984, Linda was seen on the CBS-TV special "Salute To Lady Liberty." The two-hour variety special was a star-studded salute to the Statue Of Liberty, about to undergo two years of restoration. Linda was certainly in good company that evening, as her co-stars included Frank Sinatra, Kirk Douglas, Kenny Rogers, Liza Minnelli, Ray Charles, the Charlie Daniels Band, Ben Vereen, Brooke Shields, Marie Osmond, Louis Jourdan, Tony Orlando, Emmanuel Lewis, Betty Buckley, and the Dallas Cowboys Cheerleaders.

Throughout the first year of her divorce, Linda enjoyed her new-found freedom to come and go as she pleased. She was free to devote her time to attending public functions, going to fashion shows, and posing for several high-fashion magazine layouts. For the first time in years her schedule, apart from the show, was entirely up to her. Her kids were busy with school, and she could indulge herself with all of the things that she loved to do.

One of her greatest passions had always been fashion shows. After all, her start in show business had come as a result of a fashion show she had attended when she was eighteen years old. In December of 1983 she flew to New York City to attend Diana Vreeland's annual costume exhibit gala at the Metropolitan Museum Of Art. That special affair was attended by several other movie and television stars, including Claudette Colbert, Carol Burnett, and Amy Irving, dressed in lavish designer gowns. Not only did Linda sweep into the glamorous party wearing a stunning Bob Mackie original—she entered with Mackie on her arm as her escort! As the flashbulbs exploded around her that night, and she flashed her famous smile for the cameras, it was evident that a new Linda Gray had arrived on the scene. Her divorce had just become final; now she was calling all the shots. She was in total control of her life, and it was obvious that night that she was enjoying every minute of it.

★ 8 ★
Linda Gray vs. Sue Ellen

The seventh regular season of "Dallas," which began in the fall of 1984, offered several fresh challenges to the formula of the show. According to the Nielsen Ratings, "Dallas" was one of the hottest shows in television history. It had been the Number One rated fictional show in the past four seasons of broadcasting. It was officially Number One in three out of four of those seasons, with only the news program "60 Minutes" leading "Dallas" by nine-tenths of a rating point in the 1982–1983 season.

How long could "Dallas" maintain its viewer popularity in the face of cast changes and stiff competition from its fast-rising competitors? The 1983–1984 television season assuredly marked the peak in popularity of the prime-time soap operas, with "Dallas" rated Number One, "Dynasty" at Number Three, "Falcon Crest" rated Number Seven, and "Knots Landing" trailing at Number Eleven, (based on rating points for the entire broadcast season).

In 1984 Barbara Bel Geddes' failing health and subsequent heart surgery left the producers of "Dallas" in a quandary: should they kill off the character of Miss Ellie, or should they attempt to recast the role with a different actress? And if they chose the latter course, who could they find as a believable replacement for Bel Geddes—and would the audience accept her unquestioningly? Ultimately it was decided that the character of Miss Ellie gave the show a sense of stability. With both Ewing parents missing from the plot of the show, there would be no one left to exert parental control and occasionally shame J.R. into facing up to his spoiled childishness and greed. Miss Ellie's ability to put J.R. in his place for acting like such a jerk was an aspect of the show that helped to make J.R. more than a one-dimensional, cardboard villain. With this in mind, veteran TV-star Donna Reed was hired to replace Barbara Bel Geddes as Miss Ellie.

At the time, Linda Gray expressed her admiration for Reed's courage in stepping into a role, knowing that every minute the viewers would be comparing her to her predecessor. It was also during this particular broadcast season that Linda really began to make it known that she was not 100 percent thrilled by what Sue Ellen was up to on the show. Gray was becoming dismayed by the fact that Sue Ellen's only emotional release seemed to come from a glass filled with ice cubes and an ample shot of Scotch whiskey.

While filming the 1984–1985 season, Linda found that she had very little control over the writers' continuation of Sue Ellen's chronic drinking. But she was well aware that this was the last year of her existing contract on the show. When the seventh season was finished filming, she would be in a better position to negotiate for more agreeable terms, both for the character of Sue Ellen and for herself as an actress.

In hopes of keeping Gray and co-star Victoria Principal happy with their working situation on the show, the producers and writers devised a plot twist that would have the characters of Sue Ellen and Pam traveling to the Far East and enabling both actresses to have an on-location, expenses-paid holiday. Naturally, both Victoria and Linda found this most agreeable, and they had a great time in the Orient.

One of the real problems that Linda personally found in the seventh season was her growing fear that, as an actress, she made such a convincing drunk that the audience would think that she actually had a substance abuse problem. "When I first started playing her," she explained, "because she was psychotic and a drunk, I expected people to react negatively to her. I didn't expect her to be welcomed into people's homes. So I decided to make her a little more vulnerable. But anything I did was acceptable. People forgave me because I was married to such an S.O.B. [J.R.]. There I was expecting the worst and I wound up getting accolades." After finishing the seventh season, Linda was less accepting of Sue Ellen's woes.

"I don't want any more of this!" she protested at the end of the 1984–1985 season. "That'll be it! I've told Lorimar that I'm through with drinking in the series. I won't do it! Frankly, I was bored last year. At the time I renegotiated my contract, I complained that all I did was sit around. As an actress it was not challenging nor fulfilling. I figured that before I reached the point of hating my job, I should speak up!"

With the opening of the seventh season of "Dallas," Afton discovers Bobby's body in J.R.'s office—shot with a bullet obviously meant for J.R. Bobby is hospitalized and left in stable condition, but he has lost his eyesight. By the next episode, the identity of his assailant remains a mystery, but Sue Ellen is the prime suspect, according to J.R. He realizes how mad he has made her by having framed Peter on the false cocaine charge, and he is convinced that she was out to kill him.

The gun is eventually found in the town house of Cliff Barnes, and he is arrested for attempted murder. However, it is later revealed that Cliff and Pam's sister, Katherine Wentworth, shot Bobby out of jealousy— thinking that if she couldn't have him, no one would. For years Katherine had been madly in love with Bobby—a love that made her murderously insane. Her futile attempts at stealing him from Pam had finally gotten the best of her. Katherine is arrested, Bobby regains his sight, and estranged Ewing cousin Jamie (actress Jennilee Harrison) arrives at South Fork from Alaska.

J.R. suspects that Jamie is a fraud, looking to stake her claim to the Ewing fortune. He urges Sue Ellen to spy on Jamie to uncover her true identity. But instead of spying on Jamie, Sue Ellen believes the girl and begins to take her under her wing. In her protectiveness of Jamie, Sue Ellen goes as far as taking her to Jenna Wade's boutique to purchase her a brand-new wardrobe. Taking an interest in this girl whom her husband hates gives Sue Ellen a meaningful new pastime.

Seven episodes into the season Miss Ellie and Clayton return from their honeymoon, with Donna Reed introduced in the role of the family matriarch.

While Bobby and Jenna move toward setting a wedding date, Pam becomes convinced that Mark Graison is still alive. She begins a search of every clinic on the globe boasting miracle cures for incurable diseases, hoping to locate him, and refuses to give up until she does.

During the season, several new characters were integrated into the action. They included Naldo Marchetta (actor Daniel Pilon), who is Jenna's first husband; Mandy Winger (actress Deborah Shelton) who is Cliff's girlfriend and then J.R.'s mistress; and Jack Ewing (actor Dack Rambo) who is Jamie's long-lost brother. As the season progresses, Sue Ellen gets Jamie a job at Ewing Oil, Naldo torments Jenna, and Jamie finds a document that confirms her claim as a Ewing and ownership of a portion of Ewing Oil. Jamie eventually marries Cliff, uniting with him to fight J.R., and Sue Ellen accompanies Pam to Hong Kong on her search for Mark Graison.

Slimy con-man Naldo kidnaps Charlie, and he threatens Jenna. If she doesn't call off her wedding to Bobby, she will never see her daughter again. It is the day of her wedding, and she leaves Bobby "standing at the altar." When Naldo attempts to rape Jenna, she shoots him in self-defense. J.R. tries to patch up his marriage with Sue Ellen but she tells him to forget it. In turn, J.R. begins a shameless and very public affair with Mandy.

When young John Ross III is stricken with appendicitis, Sue Ellen is nowhere to be found. Confronted with the news of her son's emergency upon returning from a routine afternoon in town, J.R. accuses her of being an incompetent mother. Sue Ellen promptly begins drinking again.

Lucy Ewing falls in love again with her ex-husband Mitch, and they are wed in the season's final episode. At their wedding reception, Sue Ellen is a little too enthusiastic in toasting the bride and groom, and she passes out totally drunk. Bobby takes Pam back to her house after the wedding and spends a romantic night there; they discover that they are still madly in love. The next morning as he is leaving, he is savagely run over by a car driven by Pam's crazed sister, Katherine Wentworth. It was actually Katherine's plan to run over Pam, but Bobby pushes Pam out of the path of the car and ends up the victim instead. Wentworth's plan really backfires when she inadvertently crashes her automobile and is killed as well. In the final scene of the season, the family is gathered around Bobby's hospital bed as he dies.

The end of the seventh season finds Sue Ellen once again firmly in the grip of alcoholism. Linda Gray was determined to see some changes made before signing her next two-year contract to continue on the show. She stated with strong conviction when she began the eighth season of "Dallas" that she was all through playing Sue Ellen as a victim of the bottle. The producers bowed to her demands, and Sue Ellen began her ascent from the depths of alcoholism.

That Linda Gray was so totally adamant in her refusal to continue portraying Sue Ellen as a drunk raises the question: was there more to the story than met the eye? Has Gray ever had a problem with liquor in real life? She admits that at one point in her life, it *almost* became a problem, but she didn't allow it to get the best of her.

"I did a little too much drinking. I couldn't talk to my husband. I was afraid that nobody loved me and I wanted everybody to," says Linda, recalling the trying times before she went into therapy and began pursuing her acting career in the early 1970s. "I was not pleased to be drinking, but it was a release. It was like I had to do something, and I didn't know why. My psychiatrist said, 'It was like pouring water into a cup that was already overflowing.' I couldn't communicate because I was afraid that if I told my husband, he would leave me." It was after her three years of therapy that she found she no longer needed even to consider drinking as a problem.

Linda remembers something she said once in reply to a question from a journalist after she had become a television star on "Dallas," which led to an erroneous report that she was a heavy drinker. Says Gray, "A magazine writer asked me what I did to relax after working and taking care of the children, my ranch, and husband [this was before their divorce]. I told him I had a couple glasses of wine with my husband before dinner. That did it!"

The eighth season on "Dallas" was the one that came to be known as the "dream season." It was during this season that Sue Ellen hit her lowest point on the show and from there gradually overcame her drinking problem. The character of Bobby was dead, Barbara Bel Geddes returned to the show as Miss Ellie, Pam found Mark Graison, and Dusty Farlow returned to help Sue Ellen with her problems. However, for Linda Gray this was, more importantly, the season in which she made her directing debut. This had become the major point in the list of demands Linda made before signing her next two-year contract for the show.

According to her, if the producers of the show didn't

allow her to direct at least one episode each season, she would leave the show. This really put the producers at Lorimar in an awkward position. Bobby had been killed off because of actor Patrick Duffy's desire to leave the show. Could "Dallas" withstand the loss of *two* key characters and still maintain its position in the ratings? Initially, Lorimar's producers decided to let her quit and face the prospect of their first season without Sue Ellen.

"We can't let *her* direct!" was Lorimar's response to Linda's demands. According to Linda, she was not only hurt—she was very mad: "My anger wasn't as a feminist, it was as a human being who had dedicated seven years to the show." Larry Hagman, Patrick Duffy, and Steve Kanaly had all been allowed to direct episodes of "Dallas," and she was determined to become the first woman cast member to have the same opportunity.

"I'd paid my dues," she argued, "and that made me see not only red, but green and yellow and purple and orange! I went crazy and said, 'O.K., I'm leaving.' So they fired me. Nobody knows this, but for two weeks, I didn't have a job! They fired me. It was incomprehensible. But I said, 'Great—their loss!' When Larry Hagman heard what had been done to me, he had a meeting with the show's producers."

Had it not been for Hagman's intervention, the show might have entered its eighth season without Linda Gray as Sue Ellen Ewing. After two weeks, the producers reversed their decision, and Linda was destined to have one of her greatest goals fulfilled: she was going to direct.

Linda loved her experience directing her first episode. But, when it was time for the action to begin, she admits, "I was terrified!" The thing that impressed her most was how *different* things looked from the other side of the camera. "I did a couple of scenes and found myself in front of the cameras waiting for someone else to shout, 'Cut!' Then it hit me that *I* was the director, and *I* had to be the one to say it. That was a little difficult. But after I'd done my scenes on camera, I changed out of Sue Ellen's fancy clothes, put on sweats, tied my hair back in a ponytail and went to work."

For Linda, her first directing assignment was "a creative personal high that Larry helped me achieve. I had to perform, and I knew all eyes were on me. I had already learned a lot from being on the show, but to prepare, I went to UCLA and studied directing every Saturday morning."

According to her, it was, "one of the most exciting, challenging things I've ever done. It's a man's business, directing, and I've never understood why. I wanted to prove something, and I think I have. My episode has a different look, I think, from the usual look of the show.

"By the end of the week, I was a zombie, but filled with adrenaline. I had a great rapport with the actors. It was a loving, sharing experience," She proudly recalls. "I did it well. I did it on time. I did it under budget. They know I'm not a bit of fluff, a pretty face who doesn't know anything. They respect me and I earned that respect. That's the best kind."

The opening to the eighth season of "Dallas" was naturally Bobby Ewing's funeral. All of the characters in the cast were in total shock over the death of Bobby. Before the actual funeral takes place, things have to be put in order. Miss Ellie, as always, is the only character who seems to have any true inner strength. She is in shock, but she is still able to put her grief on hold long enough to plan the funeral. Pam is inconsolable, and Sue Ellen chooses her favorite solution to any problem—she heads straight for the nearest bar.

Linda agreed that Sue Ellen had to hit rock bottom before she could rid herself of her dependency on drink. According to Gray, "They had to bottom me out before I could begin to move forward. The first script came in. 'Hmmm,' I thought as I read it. Then the second script, and they had Sue Ellen drinking with a bag lady. 'At least this is acting,' I thought. I've always been someone who would rather play an interesting character than someone who was liked and safe."

The plotline found fashionable Sue Ellen Ewing, former socialite, waking up on skid row, drinking cheap Muscatel with the bums. It was really one of the most entertaining sequences in which Linda Gray had been seen in quite some time. She was really able to let go and play the character as a disheveled mess. "What I love about it was the make-up," laughed Linda. "I used to have to spend up to two hours with someone dabbing my face and fixing my hair. Suddenly, I'm out in twenty minutes. They would smear some black under my eyes, rub baby oil in my hair, and say, 'She's ready.' It was fabulous! I dreaded it when they started making me pretty again."

For the first several months of the 1985–1986 season, each of the characters, in their own way, comes to grips with Bobby's death. One of the first matters of business to be taken care of is the reading of Bobby's will. J.R. of course goes into a shocked rage when he finds out that Bobby has left all of his shares of Ewing Oil stock to his son Christopher—meaning that control of half of the company now rests in Pam's hands.

When Sue Ellen suddenly disappears, an extensive search for her is launched. She is finally found in a bed in the detox unit of the city hospital. J.R. and Dusty engage in a huge fist fight right there in the drunk ward over who is ultimately going to take care of her. The outcome is that J.R. has her committed to a sanitarium again.

Much to Pam's shock, Mark Graison shows up in Dallas—alive and well. The doctors in Hong Kong have miraculously saved his life. He has returned just when she needs him most. Sue Ellen also eventually begins to find inspiration in Mark. After she has reached her lowest point, she somehow finds the strength to stop drinking. She dries out successfully, and begins to work with Mark as a volunteer at his new medical research facility, Graison Research.

Since she is the legal proxy for her son's share of Ewing Oil, Pam begins showing up at the company's office every day, to carry out Bobby's work. This really infuriates J.R.! Willing to do anything to drive Pam away from him and Ewing Oil, J.R. comes up with a scheme to have her invest all of her time, money, and energy in a bogus emerald mine in South America. He enlists the services of a man named Matt Cantrell (actor Mark Singer) to lead her on a wild goose chase. Jenna gets involved with Jack Ewing, Donna discovers that she is pregnant, and J.R. becomes involved with a devious but devastatingly beautiful woman named Angelica Nero (actress Barbara Carrera).

Now that she is in control of her drinking problem, Sue Ellen is uncertain as to what she is going to do with her life. When her mother, the nosey Patricia Shepard (actress Martha Scott), comes to town to help her daughter out, Sue Ellen temporarily moves in with her. J.R.'s affair with Mandy Winger reaches its pinnacle, and Dusty wants Sue Ellen to come to live with him. Sue Ellen decides against it.

By the end of the season, Pam marries Mark, Sue Ellen and J.R. reconcile, and Angelica Nero puts everyone's life in danger. It seems she wants to kill Jack and J.R., so she rigs two separate bombs: one in Jack's car, and one in J.R.'s office at Ewing Oil. However, her plan backfires. As the two bombs explode, Jamie is in Jack's car, and Sue Ellen is in J.R.'s office.

In the final sequence of the eighth season, Pam awakens on the morning after her wedding to Mark Graison. Hearing water running, she walks into the bathroom and, opening the door of the shower stall, is greeted by none other than Bobby Ewing! Is she hallucinating? What happens to Sue Ellen and Jamie? Thus ends the eighth season of "Dallas"—with perhaps the most puzzling cliffhanger yet.

"Dallas" has built a reputation for bringing its viewers the unexpected, but the end of this particular season presented new challenges. After fans of "Dallas" all over the world had seen Bobby Ewing killed by a speeding car only a year before, how on earth would the writers bring him back to life? As that cliffhanger episode, appropriately entitled "Blast From The Past," demonstrated brilliantly, one should always expect the most surprising developments on "Dallas."

When Patrick Duffy had opted to quit the show the season before, Linda Gray commented, "Life is made up of choices. He made his. If the series, now in its eighth year, had been at the bottom of the ratings, I, too, might have thought it was time to leave. But I couldn't see quitting a series this successful."

Because Larry Hagman had intervened in the contract negotiations between Gray and Lorimar, instead of being absent from the show that season, Linda found herself in an even stronger position than before. She received a great deal of publicity and praise for her directing debut, and she was happier about her role on the show than she had been in previous seasons.

Larry continued to be Linda's greatest admirer. He glowingly stated, "She has proved she can play anything: a psychotic, an alcoholic, the rejected woman, the woman on the edge of promiscuity, the woman having problems with her mother and sister, the woman who deals with the infatuation of a boy less than half her age."

According to "Dallas" producer Leonard Katzman, "We've actually nearly run out of severe emotional problems for her to handle!" The show's ninth season would see the growth of Sue Ellen into someone as conniving and clever as J.R. himself.

As the show went into its 1986 hiatus, Linda found that she was loving her life on both sides of the camera. She had finally gotten her feet wet as a director, and she couldn't wait for her next shot at the task. Her relationship with Paul Constanza was progressing smoothly, and her relationship with her children was wonderfully rewarding. Her life was no longer a case of Linda Gray vs. Sue Ellen Ewing . . . they were both getting their lives together and emerging as winners!

★ 9 ★

Fabulous
at Forty

"I have a lot more confidence in myself now!" claims
Linda Gray. And, according to her, she's not getting
any older—just better: "When people ask me how old
I am, I tell them I have the energy of a twenty-seven-
year-old," she said recently.

"I'm just not an age-oriented person," says Linda.
"So many women get hung up on growing older, but
what are you gonna do about it? Laugh . . . and keep
the moisturizer flowing!" she proclaims with a smile.

Although she turned forty-seven in 1987, Linda
isn't one of those actresses from the Zsa Zsa Gabor
school of lying about her age. In fact, she gets a charge
from the fact that her former "Dallas" co-star, Victoria
Principal is obssessed with subtracting years from her
birth certificate. Principal admits to being thirty-six;
other sources claim that she is at least forty-two.

Linda distinctly recalls being invited to Victoria's

"thirtieth" birthday party at least three years in a row. "Finally it dawned on me," laughs Linda. "'Victoria,' I said, 'Haven't I been here once or twice before?'"

Not only does Linda have a positive attitude about herself, but she has always been quite serious about taking care of herself as well. Her own personal routine is one of total health-consciousness and body maintenance. She doesn't go for fad diets or exercise binges. Her daily regime calls for consistent dietary guidelines, regular exercise, and a strong fashion sense. Her way of life is obviously beneficial, because she always looks smashingly fit, and projects the aura of a person who is genuinely enjoying life.

"It's impossible to be an actress and not take care of yourself," Linda explains. "My schedule is more hectic now than it's ever been. You have to work on your emotional well-being as well as your physical health."

What is Linda Gray's secret to looking and feeling great after the age of forty? Obviously this isn't something that she has just begun working on. Let's take her plan for a fuller life one step at a time: diet, exercise, and clothing and make-up tips.

According to Linda, one of her favorite sources of information regarding diet and nutrition has been the field of holistic medicine. "It has been a savior for me," she says, recalling that she has been fascinated with eating the right foods since she was a teenager. "I went to a very strict all-girls school, where I felt repressed," she revealed. "Because of my unhappiness, I ate lots of junk food. The more sweets I had, the more I craved. To get rid of the extra pounds, I abused my body with diets that didn't last. Fortunately, a girlfriend who wanted to become a nutritionist sent me to a doctor who practiced preventive medicine. I had such low energy, I was not surprised to be told that I had hypogylcemia.

"Did you know that by analyzing your hair, the mineral content of your body can be determined? My doctor took hair samples from the top of my scalp to the nape of my neck. The report came back that I was undernourished and very low in zinc. The treatment began with a two-day cleansing of organic apple juice. Every two hours I drank six ounces of half apple juice and half spring water. Then I was given a list of taboos. At first it was more severe than now, but the emphasis is placed on fresh fruits and vegetables, nourishing salads and broiled meats. No white flour or white sugar," recalls Linda.

"I've studied nutrition for about fifteen years," she says. "There was a time I was really fanatical about it. It was getting ridiculous. I was making the kids eat seven-grain cereals, studying nutritionist Adele Davis, and taking lots of vitamins."

Nowadays, Linda claims that she has taken what she learned about nutrition during her "fanatical" phase, and she has applied it to her own schedule, and her own realistic needs. On the set of "Dallas," you would never see Linda munching on candy bars or potato chips. Instead, she keeps an ample supply of carrots and green peppers around her as snacks. This keeps her blood sugar at a steady level, without bingeing on junk food.

"Of course, I still love champagne and caviar," she laughs, "and I don't believe in denying myself those things either." She even admits to a recent vacation where she let herself indulge a bit more than usual. "I went to Italy," she recalls, "and ate pasta three times a day and drank lots of that good wine. No one should go to that country and eat celery stalks, for heaven's sake! It would be obscene. But when I got back to the States I was very careful. I cut back on everything.

"I'm on a very personalized program," says Linda of her day-to-day dietary rules. "For me diet just means eating sensibly. Some lean meat, but mostly chicken and fish for protein, vegetables, lots of salads. Not too much bread or starchy stuff. Lots of pure water. No salt, very little sugar.

"I'm never going to follow a diet full of rigid do's and don't's. I can eyeball appropriate amounts of food on my plate. And I simply carry around a two-liter bottle of Evian water. When I've finished it, I know I've drunk my water for the day. I literally threw my scales away a couple of years ago. I focus on muscle tone and my overall shape. I know how I'm doing because of the way my clothes fit, the way I feel. In fact, I have a pair of skin-tight blue jeans that I'd never wear in public. They're my barometer. Along with a full-length mirror!"

According to her, the proper diet is only part of her fitness policy. Linda feels that you need to team that with a sensible program of regular exercise. "Eating properly and exercising," she says, "for me these things are a matter of survival. Everything works together. If you get enough exercise, your metabolism stabilizes, you have more energy, you don't tend to binge."

One of Linda's secrets for not getting into a rut and losing patience with any one exercise routine is to vary her activities. She was heavily into jogging some years ago, but then shifted to swimming. "Now I'm swimming every day," she explains, "and what I did to make it both relaxing and great exercise was to get a snorkel and mask. I find that using that equipment makes it less strenuous and I can keep going half an hour. I always hated jogging. Not only is it boring, [but] it is very jarring for a woman's body. I had fallen into doing it just like everyone else, but now I'm delighted with the way I feel after I swim."

At one point she even began playing polo. She took lessons with instructor Buzz Welker who teaches at the Eldorado Polo Club. To protect herself, she wore a face mask, just in case. "I didn't want a mallet attached to my nose! All I was doing was missing the ball," she explained. She discovered that it was much more difficult than it looks. "You have to hit it much earlier than you think. I'm not a killer competitor. When I play I like to *play*." Laughs Gray, "Sue Ellen wouldn't get out there. She'd sit in an air-conditioned box, sipping Perrier and looking at fashions. Playing polo would mess up her make-up!"

Her usual work-out is relatively simple. Linda explains, "I do a combination of yoga and calisthenics. I have this device, invented by Wayne White, that tones every part of your body. It works like big rubber bands that you pull or push. It costs about three hundred dollars, but you really don't have to have the machine. When I travel, I just use whatever's handy as a weight. I do arm exercises holding books or soup cans. If there's no barre handy, I stretch out on the floor or hold a chair.

After her 1985 trip to Singapore she also added another exercise routine. "I took up jumping rope a while ago; it's the only item I could think of to take along on a Far East tour so that I could exercise daily. Well, now I've gotten to the point where I can jump rope *on* the mini-trampoline! It's a bit of a killer, but it's superb exercise."

She goes on, "When I was staying in a Singapore hotel, I'd jump rope in front of the TV each morning. When that got monotonous, I'd do it while staring out the window. In Bangkok, I worked out on the beach. Taking care of your body has to be enjoyable, or you'll give up. If boredom sets in, alter something—either the activity or the view."

According to her, when she first achieved fame on "Dallas," she could really feel the pressures mounting, and her exercise helped her deal with the demands her new responsibilities placed on her. "At first I didn't know how to handle it," she says. "I felt I was under a gigantic microscope. But I was determined not to be changed for the worse by the experience. So I went into psychotherapy to really analyze myself. And I exercised. I know it sounds trite, but cycling and riding horseback and playing tennis really helped me burn off some of the frustrations I was feeling."

As far as her hair and make-up are concerned, these days she likes to keep things simple. Explains Linda, "I love to have a tan body, but never my face. I collect wonderful straw hats and visors, always drink tons of water and wear a sunscreen—even under make-up." For her hairstyle, she's said that she prefers a body wave and a simple layered cut: "There's no curl, just wave. And I can wash it, blow it dry, or simply let it dry naturally and arrange it with my fingers. It's great, because of the freedom from fussing. They fuss enough with me on the set.

"I love make-up!" she exclaims. "It's fun to experiment. But I don't try to hide behind it. Make-up can't make you beautiful. It can just make you prettier. I have nothing against that. I just think that what's inside is more important. I have to admit, I love eye make-up because I think my eyes are my strong point. As you grow older, you will have lines and things you can't hide. Don't try. The most beautiful people may or may not be that physically attractive, but there is something about them that makes you think they are. That's usually love, kindness, joy, passion, sensuality, intelligence, sensitivity. A woman who has the capacity to smile easily is beautiful. A healthy woman is beautiful. A woman who can take chances and make mistakes and grow with them is beautiful."

Since all of those things can be said of Linda Gray, it's no wonder she looks so great all the time! However, she does try to keep a good sense of humor about her looks and her fame. "I make an effort when I go to an opening or an industry function that's being covered by newspapers all over the world. But then, they can always get that shot of you in mid-sentence or mid-blink when you look stupid anyway. That's where having a sense of humor comes in."

Linda admits that one of her biggest passions is fashion. She has a real sense of style and a sense of what works for her. She prefers to wear earth tones: sand, beige, rust, browns, greens, and oranges. She claims that she is "not a pastels person. I always start with rich earth tones. That's true for my environment, too. Earthy tones just feel good to me."

Although she feels comfortable in casual clothes, she is quick to admit that "something happens to you when you put on high heels and a beautiful gown. You carry yourself differently . . . you feel wonderful!" According to her, her love of fashion began right after high school: "After seventeen years of uniforms, I went wild over clothes!" Her favorite designers include Calvin Klein, Georgio Armani, and Perry Ellis. When she wants to slip into something really glamorous she turns to designer-to-the-stars Bob Mackie. Says Linda, "He does what he does better than anybody in the business. Bob has that wonderful way of making a woman look absolutely magnificent. He minimizes her flaws and maximizes her good points. I put on his clothes and I go! I just feel terrific."

One of Linda's fashion secrets is to mix and match outfits. She'll take one designer's jacket, and wear it with another designer's skirt, or maybe a pair of leather pants. "I like looking different—I've been exposed to a lot of fashion, and by now I've developed an individual style."

One of the designers on the set of "Dallas" who is responsible for Linda Gray's "Sue Ellen" clothes is Bill Travilla. Travilla became famous for designing the dress that Marilyn Monroe wore in the film *The Seven Year Itch*—the dress that billowed upward when she stood over the subway grating. Speaking of the way he likes to dress Sue Ellen for her fashionable, highly monied events, Travilla explains, "Sue Ellen wears hats. She dresses well to go to the city. I dress Sue Ellen in a very sensuous way. I think she's silk charmeuse—luscious!"

Now that we know how Linda stays in shape, her secrets for looking glamorous, let's find out how it is that she seems to keep getting sexier all the time. "Being sexy has nothing to do with the outside of a woman," Linda claims. "Women who have the most sex appeal are those who enjoy life, who take pleasure in themselves and who live according to their own rules—and not those imposed by others. This type of woman is attractive to both men and women. Their secret is that they love life.

"The most important thing is to never stop growing, and never stop enjoying. And don't wish that you had done something at another time in your life. Any time is the right time if you make it so. No one tells a rose when to bloom!" Her strategy must work, because Linda Gray is certainly one of the most beautiful blossoms ever to have graced a television screen!

★ 10 ★

New Directions

The ninth season of "Dallas" brought several significant changes for Linda Gray. Not only did the character of Sue Ellen reach a new peak of development, but Linda's directing career progressed as well. Her sharp and insightful direction on her second contractually guaranteed "Dallas" assignment that season led to an offer to direct an episode of another television show—"Mike Hammer." It was the fulfillment of a dream for her—she was really being taken seriously as a director.

When the 1986–1987 season began, it was common knowledge that Patrick Duffy was returning to "Dallas," but the big question was how the writers would explain it in the plot of the show. Duffy had originally left the show to pursue other acting offers. But after he obtained his freedom, he found that the

opportunities were more sparse than he had antici-
pated.

Ratings were another factor that influenced Patrick
Duffy to rejoin the cast. "Dallas" had been rated
the Number Two show in its seventh season
(1984–1985), but it had slipped to Number Six in the
ratings during its eighth season (1985–1986). The
producers at Lorimar—and Larry Hagman himself—
convinced Patrick to return to the show. Lorimar and
Hagman felt that, without Bobby, a key element in the
show's chemistry was missing. The character of J. R.
Ewing seemed even more conniving when compared
to his charming and fair-dealing younger brother.
When the character of Bobby died, this source of family tension was lost.

After the negotiations with Patrick Duffy were completed, Lorimar announced the return of Bobby
Ewing. The producers also explained their rationale
for bringing him back: it was hoped that he would
help save the show's sagging ratings. This announcement rubbed several cast members the wrong way—
particularly Linda Gray. She was insulted and hurt
that the efforts of the rest of the cast were so crassly
disregarded and that Duffy was being viewed as the
show's "savior."

According to Linda, "For me, to be told that he is
coming to save the show after all of us had paid our
dues didn't set well. It's nothing against Patrick. It has
nothing to do with him personally. But I thought,
'What kind of slap is this?' We weren't doing badly.
We went into a little decline," she said in reference to
the ratings, "but we certainly didn't fall to sixty-
fourth!"

Linda was also unhappy about certain statements that the show's producer, Leonard Katzman, had made to the press. She felt Katzman had insulted the women cast members when he stressed the importance of the men on the show: "I have said to anyone who will listen that I believe 'Dallas' is a show of strong men—not weak women—but strong men. But in the long run, the people who produce the show have to be responsible for the direction it takes, not the actors who may not be as concerned with the overall feel of the show."

Linda, quite unamused by Katzman's comments, quickly replied: "I've gotten patted on the head so many times and told, 'It's an ensemble show, and go to your room and don't come out.' Well, that's great. That really is terrific. But there comes a time when you say, 'Wait a minute. I'm not going to my room, and I'm not going to be quiet.' I was offended and frustrated by what he said—and took the stand that if that's the way it's going to be, maybe it's time for me to move on.

"The cards are on the table," she said. "I'm not getting the stimulation I need as an actress. [I] can't stagnate. I would rather take a risk. I'd rather do a play on Broadway. I'd rather go to Europe and do film. I'd rather see the outback in a jeep in Australia. My life is waiting to happen. I'm re-evaluating a lot of things. It's been very mellowing, very secure, much more an in-touch-with-self year than I've ever had. This is a new part of my life and I'm in charge. I'm in control. And I call all the shots.

"This will be a shock, but it makes me feel good, because most of the time that I talk it is very superficial. But what good happens in life that doesn't get started by a little jolt?" No doubt Linda's comments gave the people at Lorimar a bit of a jolt, and her situation as an actress—and as a director—promptly improved.

After she had stated her case she admitted, "Everyone was very upset by my stand, which is very strange. They freaked out. But they did hear me—and they are trying to make me happy."

According to her, she had grown tired of Sue Ellen Ewing "going from one affair to another, from one drinking crisis to the next. Every time I've said that, they've literally patted me on the head—and then it would be the same old thing again: affairs and drinking, drinking and affairs. I'm tired of playing the victim. I need to grow as an actress and a woman. And I've made that point very strongly this season."

By the ninth show of the season, she was much more content with Sue Ellen's role in the plotlines. "She is showing some growth—she becomes conniving and funny. So they are listening to me," Linda said at that time. Indeed, Sue Ellen had some of he best antics during season nine.

"It will be a great year for me. I'm almost like a female J.R. this year, but not evil," she explained as the shows began airing in the autumn of 1986. "I'm a little conniving, a little devious, a lot funny—it's everything I've wanted. I guess I'd done the drunk role so convincingly for so long that they thought I was so good at it, and they'd just keep doing it. People really thought that's who I was. Finally, after nine years, I'm getting to do something I always wanted to do. They're changing Sue Ellen!"

The opening episode of the 1986–1987 season was one of the most watched shows in "Dallas" history.

One of the last things to happen on the show the previous spring had been Pam's wedding to the long-lost Mark Graison. But when Pam opens the shower door on the morning after their wedding, there stands Bobby Ewing under the running water! How would his return be explained? Unbelievable as it seemed, everything that had happened during the entire eighth season was now being dismissed simply as Pam's bad dream. It was as though Bobby's getting run over by Katherine Wentworth's car, the reappearance of Mark Graison, the evil deeds of Angelica Nero, and the impending deaths of Jamie and Sue Ellen were all just scenes from a nightmare.

This explanation meant that all of the plot twists from the previous season were undone, and the situations were back to where they had been at the close of season seven: Mark Graison was still missing and presumed dead, Donna was still pregnant, there was no Angelica Nero, and Sue Ellen was still a drunk. It also meant that Jamie Ewing Barnes hadn't been blown up in Jack's car, and Sue Ellen hadn't wandered into J.R.'s office just as the bomb intended for him exploded.

As the season progressed, Bobby decides to remarry Pam, Jenna discovers that she is pregnant by Bobby, Donna enters the political arena by getting involved in a senatorial oil lobby in Washington, D.C., and a man named Wes Parmalee (actor Steve Forrest)— masquerading as the late Jock Ewing—arrives in Dallas. Early in the season, Sue Ellen makes a vow to quit drinking once and for all, and she begins to work out in the South Fork gym to get in shape. Her plan is to really "get her act" together"—so "together" in fact, that J.R. will eventually be insane to have her back as his wife. However, she must first get J.R.'s mistress, Mandy Winger, out of the way. She proceeds to hatch one of the cleverest and most elaborate schemes of their entire seventeen-year marriage.

Sue Ellen's plan is to make Mandy appear as a common, low-class tart in J.R.'s eyes. One day while Sue Ellen is shopping in the local shopping mall, she happens across a boutique called Valentine Lingerie that sells sexy negligees and frilly underwear, à la Frederick's of Hollywood. After purchasing the store and becoming the controlling head of the entire operation, she devises an intricate scheme to launch a huge advertising campaign featuring a beautiful model, clad in an almost non-existent outfit. As part of her master plan, Sue Ellen sees to it, through agents and representatives, that the role of "Valentine Girl" goes to Mandy Winger. So that no one in Dallas knows what she is up to, she retains the store's original owner, Oswald Valentine (actor Derek McGrath) as a 10 percent owner, and visible "front man."

Not only will Mandy appear in the store's advertisements but she will also star in the steamy Valentine Lingerie mail-order catalogue. To top it off, Sue Ellen sells Mandy's Valentine contract to a filmmaker who intends to feature her in X-rated movies. Sue Ellen knows how J.R. will burn when he sees photos of his mistress gracing girlie calendars and magazine foldouts. She also knows that J.R. will be turned off if Mandy wishes to concentrate on a career.

The plan works beautifully. Mandy has a huge argument with J.R., and he gives her an ultimatum. She must choose: the X-rated movie offer or her relationship with him. After Mandy signs the papers to begin the movie career she has always dreamed of—in faraway Hollywood—Sue Ellen reveals that she was the one controlling Valentine Lingerie and that Mandy has just fallen into her trap.

That particular scene was a terrific turning point, both for Linda Gray the actress, and for the character of Sue Ellen Ewing. It afforded Linda her best opportunity yet to use the full expressive value of her famous eyes, and allowed Sue Ellen to mastermind a caper that rivaled J.R.'s most devious manipulations.

According to Linda, close-up scenes such as her confrontation with Mandy Winger are really the ones she most enjoys, especially when there is plenty of dramatic tension. "It's important for me, because I work with my eyes," she explains. "The closer the camera gets the better, because the eyes say so much without my having to *say* anything."

She claims that when she does a scene, she thinks of the TV camera as "a friend I know is there and I ignore. I'm aware it's there, but when I work I have to connect with the other actor. You have to focus on who you're working with or what you're doing."

In December of 1986, Linda again took her place on the other side of the cameras to direct her second episode of the show. The episode was aired on February 27, 1987, and was entitled "The Nerd Gets His Revenge," referring directly to the character of Cliff Barnes and his shocking announcement that he owns a portion of Ewing Oil.

At this point in the plot, Donna Krebbs is living in Washington, D.C., Ray is beginning an affair with the pregnant Jenna, and J.R. has gotten the entire family into a real predicament. As part of a scheme to bring up the price of Texas oil, he hires a mercenary named B.D. Calhoun (actor Hunter Von Leer) to blow up several Middle Eastern oil fields. When the plan backfires, Calhoun vows vengeance, which leads to a shoot-out with J.R. Also, Jamie is killed in a mountain climbing accident in Mexico, and Jack Ewing is nowhere to be found. It seems that Jamie died without having signed the papers finalizing her divorce from Cliff Barnes. Since Jack had sold his shares of Ewing Oil stock to Jamie, Cliff now inherits their portion of the company. At this point, Jack's estranged wife, April (actress Sheree J. Wilson), has arrived in Dallas to stake her claim to the Ewing empire.

When Linda got hold of the script that she was to direct for season nine, she made some creative decisions as to how she was going to improve on the usual formula of the show. "One of my pet peeves," she explained, "is that on 'Dallas' they don't move the camera enough, so within the confines of what I had to do on my script, I wanted the camera to move and I moved it, which I think is much more exciting. I told the actors, 'I don't want you sitting at a desk and have to come in close for a tight shot.' It bores me. I've looked at our show—as an audience, as an actress, as a camera, as a director. I moved the camera as a director, and I'm proud of it. By moving the camera it makes the audience feel like a participant. You feel like you're really there when the people are eating breakfast."

In the plot of "The Nerd Gets His Revenge," Sue Ellen is searching for the new Valentine Girl. Ray is fighting for custody of the baby Donna is carrying, J.R. accuses Pam of spying for Cliff, Miss Ellie contemplates selling South Fork, and Cliff plays his trump card by announcing that he has legally inherited Jamie's estate—and with it, a portion of Ewing Oil.

Indeed, there is a noticeable stylistic difference in the look of the episode Linda directed. From zooming upward pans of skyscrapers as location identification, to sweeping dolly shots of the restaurant at the Oil Baron's Club, a variety of camera angles and a strong visual sense of the action are evident throughout. There is one scene in which Sue Ellen and Pam are at the shooting of a Valentine Lingerie ad. While the two ladies are having their conversation, a series of shapely legs walk by them on the elevated ramp in the foreground; the viewer sees nothing but legs from the top of the TV screen to the bottom. Another highly effective scene takes place at the apartment of April Stevens. In the beginning of the scene, all of the dialogue is heard over a close-up shot of the fine crystal glasses and decanters that April is using to mix drinks for J.R. and herself.

Those on the set were quite impressed with Linda's second directing assignment. According to Sheree J. Wilson, who plays the part of April, "When Linda directed [her] episode, she must have baked for a week. She brought in homemade muffins and cookies every day. [She's] so nice you can't believe she's real!" That's typical of Linda: she wasn't busy enough directing her co-workers from behind the camera, she also baked for them all week too! It was her show, and she was in her glory.

Little more than a week after Linda's second episode as a director aired it was announced that she had been asked to direct an episode of the "Mike Hammer" television series. Negotiations were underway between Gray and the "Mike Hammer" production staff when poor ratings caused the detective series to be dropped from the fall 1987 line-up. Nonetheless, Linda was flattered to have been considered for the assignment in the first place.

Although her career as a director is just beginning, Linda has no intention of stopping at acting and directing—she plans to go into producing as well! "I would love to be in a position where I can produce," she proclaims. "It is terribly stimulating and challenging. I have my own production company, LGP Inc., which stands for Linda Gray Productions, and we're in the process of buying two books. I have books I would love to see made into movies—with or without me as an actress."

"My craft is a business for me," explains Linda of her commitment to the world of entertainment, "but it also has an attachment to my being. That takes it from being a business outside of myself to being a business incorporated with 'self.' I don't go to work from nine to five and go home and leave it. I've incorporated my business into who I am. This is what I love. This is a business. I am a business. I like who I am. I like where I'm going. I like what I've done. I can always do better. And that's why I've incorporated."

According to Linda, one of the reasons that she would like to go into production work is that there are so few good roles, and she isn't content to sit around and wait to be offered great parts. Says Linda, "It's very true that the roles for women over thirty are very minimal, and everyone wants all the roles Meryl Streep has ever done, but there aren't enough to go around. I feel now, that things are changing, that people are now aware that women in their thirties and forties have life experience to offer. These are not just pretty faces with no substance. Society's changed. I think there have been great strides and inroads for women. I think it made enough people angry enough to say, 'Wait a minute. What are we going to do, sit around and bitch and complain and moan that there aren't enough women's roles? Or do we go out and find fabulous writers who know how to write for women, who *will* write wonderful women's roles?'"

Linda claims that all of her favorite role models were women who weren't afraid to take control of their own destinies. "All the women I admire— Georgia O'Keeffe, Katharine Hepburn—never let anyone dictate their life-style. I hope I can pass that on, too, so women won't say, 'I'm thirty . . . I'm thirty-five—I can't do this.' It's all self-inflicted. You have to acknowledge your own uniqueness. What about Bette Davis? Look what she's still capable of doing!"

Now that she's gotten several chances to direct and made positive changes in her personal life, as well as her life on "Dallas" as Sue Ellen, Linda Gray feels great. "It took this gal a helluva long time to get where she is. It was one long, often arduous trip, but I enjoyed every mile. I do the best I can. I still see me as some delicious Napoleon with lots of layers all unfolding, and that's the way I like it."

In spite of all of the rumors about flaring tempers on the set of "Dallas," Linda claims that her working relationship with her co-workers is really quite friendly and congenial. "People won't believe that you really get along," explains Gray. "We all work equally hard on the series and are equally intense about our jobs. Larry is a phenomenon. He's never difficult. He's very professional. So is everyone in the cast. We don't have time for petty jealousies."

Linda singles out the man who plays her dastardly TV husband, J.R., as being in reality, her closest friend on and off the set of the show. "He's my best friend, besides my children," says Linda. "All during the time of my divorce, Larry was there for me—without fail, without questions, unconditionally. He and his lovely wife, Maj, saw me through. Larry is like the male version of me! The child, the eight-year-old in Larry—that's the one I'm really crazy about."

According to Linda, Larry gives himself a break from talking for one day each week. These are known as his "days of silence," and he generally takes them on Sundays. "I love Larry's days of silence," laughs Linda. "When he has misbehaved in his boyish way, I pick his day of silence to chew him out. I really let him have it like a common scold, while Maj just looks on approvingly and smiles. Since Larry will *never* violate his day of silence, all he can do is sit there and take it—maybe just whistling occasionally in resignation."

Linda has made several changes in her personal life. In 1986 she broke up with her steady beau, Paul Constanza, after dating him for three years. Their relationship had simply run its course. In October of that year, she began seeing twenty-six-year-old Didier Fitoussi, whom she met in Paris. However, that romance only lasted until February of 1987. By spring she was seen on the arm of a new beau, Roy Bechtol.

"It's difficult to meet men," says Linda, "but right now, that's not really the focus of my life. If I meet them, fine. But this is a wonderfully selfish, beautiful time in my life." According to her, getting involved with a man often leads to a dilemma: "You have to ask yourself, 'What do you see in this person? Do you find him supportive? Is he only going out with you because you're a celebrity? Is he just . . . looking around the restaurant, wondering who is looking at us?' Men get intimidated by my salary, and the fact that usually it's the male who's dominant in a relationship. And, yes, by the power. Because of my life-style being more reclusive than most, whenever I go out in public with somebody, it's immediately 'a romance.' And if he is any younger, that's totally blown out of proportion."

Linda is in no hurry to get involved in a permanent relationship; at the moment she is enjoying her freedom. "I have a wonderfully secure feeling that I can do anything I want to do," she says. "I don't have to ask permission from anybody. If I want to go to a party, I go. If I want to leave at ten o'clock, I'm out of there. If I want to get on a plane and go to New York, I do it. All of this is stuff that I never dreamed I could ever do without first asking permission of someone else."

Although she claims that she is still friendly with her ex-husband, Ed Thrasher, Linda does not socialize with him. She adds, however, that "when my kids get married or have babies, I want to go to those family functions without daggers across the room. He will always be their dad. I will always be their mother."

In part, she blames her own silence for deepening the schism between herself and Ed. "Because I'm so private," she explains, "I didn't say anything to the press at the time [of her divorce]. But they needed to write something, so they wrote that I dumped this faithful man because I had become a movie star. To this day, Ed believes that. And that's very, very painful to me."

According to Linda, her relationship with Paul Constanza helped to readjust to single life. She found him "delicious, delightful, a gift to me. Paul Constanza was everything my husband was not. Listen, I love sharing my life with someone. That's the way it's meant to be. But I won't settle. And I'm not looking constantly. I'm getting to know 'me.' It's a wonderful, beautiful time. Right now I'm not eager to get married again."

Although she is not interested in marriage, her daughter Kehly is. When Linda co-hosted the television broadcast of the Macy's Thanksgiving Day Parade with Larry Hagman in November of 1986, they both introduced their families on the air. When Linda presented Jeff and Kehly, she also introduced her future son-in-law (whom Kehly wed October 31, 1987).

Linda is very thankful for the positive events that have occurred in her personal life and in her fulfilling career. Several people near her have experienced tragedies. Her sister Betty lost her daughter, Lesli, in a hit-and-run car accident in the early 1980s, and in 1986 Betty underwent a mastectomy. Personal tragedy struck on the set of "Dallas," when Patrick Duffy's parents were murdered in late 1986 in their Montana tavern.

"It makes you wonder why some people are blessed with wonderful lives, and why some people end up in the gutter. Sometimes I think God gives the harder lessons to the stronger people," says Linda. "That's the confusion for me. I don't understand life; sometimes it just doesn't seem fair."

According to Gray, "God gave me this celebrity, and I can do two things with it. I can be greedy and say, 'Look how famous I am and how much money I have,' or I can ask, 'How can I give back to the universe what it's given to me?' I want to help other women, so I narrated a video that teaches women how to give themselves breast self-examinations."

Linda felt that by narrating the self-help video, *The Five-Minute Breast Self-Examination,* she was doing something that might, in some small way, save another woman from the same traumatic experience that her sister Betty lived through. (This tape can be found in libraries and medical offices across the country.)

The many growth experiences that Linda has been through in her life, inspired her to put some of her thoughts down on paper. The result is her own self-help book. "It's a book for women actually. It's called *Life: A Funny Thing,*" she explains. "Jane Fonda took care of the outside of us, my book hopefully will take care of the inner 'us.' My favorite chapter is called 'Watch Me.' It describes how all of us have gotten stumbling blocks in our careers and our lives, and whenever anyone says to me, 'You can't do that,' or 'We can't let her do that,' I say, 'Watch me!' And, so far, in every instance, I've accepted the challenge, gone after it, and have succeeded."

By the close of the ninth season of "Dallas" in May 1987, more changes were destined for the show. It had been announced early that year that Susan Howard's role of Donna Krebbs was being written out of the show. And Victoria Principal announced that she was leaving at the end of the season.

In the last episode of season nine, Pam crashes her car into a truck as she returns to South Fork from an appointment with her doctor. Senator Dowling (actor Jim McMullen) persuades Donna to stay in Washington, D.C., with him, Clayton Farlow's health is failing, and, following a governmental investigation, J.R. loses control of Ewing Oil. Meanwhile, Jenna has her baby, and Mandy Winger comes back to town to show Sue Ellen her true colors.

Since Sue Ellen's latest Valentine Lingerie sales figures have been poor, at Oswald Valentine's urging, she allows Mandy to return to Dallas for another "Valentine Girl" advertising campaign. In her final scene of the season, Sue Ellen accuses Mandy of having come back to Dallas simply to chase J.R., and states that she is of no more value to Valentine Lingerie than a "disposable piece of facial tissue." By the end of the scene, the two women are hissing hateful insults at each other. The last shot of the season shows Pam's sports car exploding and engulfed in flames.

Through all of the cast and character changes on "Dallas," Linda Gray's portrayal of Sue Ellen has remained a steady favorite of audiences worldwide. According to producer Leonard Katzman, "Wherever I go, anywhere in the world, people invariably tell me the one person they want to meet from 'Dallas' is Sue Ellen. In most places in Europe and Asia, they don't even know her real name!"

Linda has always been fascinated by the importance that the show has for people. "Some people take 'Dallas' as a farce. They love to watch it, hate it, put it down, or laugh at it. Others take each word as gospel and wouldn't miss an episode for the world."

During the 1986–1987 season (in America), "Dallas" aired Fridays at 9:00 P.M. on CBS, opposite NBC's hit show, "Miami Vice." In the ratings, "Dallas" beat the hot crime show hands down!

During the summer of 1987 it was announced that Linda would be co-starring with Kenny Rogers in the CBS made-for-TV movie "The Gambler, Part III—The Legend Continues," to be aired in two parts November 22 and 24, 1987. The previous sequel to Kenny's 1980 original film "The Gambler," entitled "The Gambler,

Part II—The Adventure Continues" (1983), became the highest-rated television-produced movie ever broadcast. Always looking for a new acting adventure, Gray was excited about the challenge of her first old-time Western.

The action in "The Gambler, Part III" picked up the exploits of gambling cowboy Brady Hawkes in the late 1800s. As she began work on the film, Linda Gray relished the break away from super-chic Sue Ellen. You can't get much further away from the role of Sue Ellen than playing the part of a pioneer woman from the last decade. She explained at the time, "They [the producers] told me I would be playing a prairie schoolteacher who carries her own water bucket." The story took place in 1889 on a Sioux Indian reservation in the Dakota territory. It was filmed in Santa Fe, New Mexico, in July and August of 1987.

For the role, Linda had to de-glamourize herself a bit. This included cutting off her fashionably long fingernails. She was quick to point out that, "Sue Ellen wasn't invited to Santa Fe, and her shoulder pads are still somewhere in Dallas!"

The tenth season of "Dallas" (1987–1988) presented a new set of challenges for the cast and crew of the show. Faced with a possible strike by the Directors Guild Of America, set for June 30, 1987, Lorimar Productions decided that it would be wise to have the first twelve episodes of the season "in the can" before the strike went into effect. Instead of taking their usual hiatus, the cast and crew remained in Dallas for a month and a half. The work was accomplished quickly and efficiently, yielding the dozen new episodes in a record-breaking eight weeks.

During the April–June "rush" schedule that spring,

Linda Gray kept especially busy, both on and off of the set. She spent a great deal of her spare time with her latest boyfriend, forty-year-old Texas businessman Roy Bechtol. She was arm-in-arm with Bechtol on April 26 when she paid a visit to the El Paso Child Crisis Center in El Paso, Texas. This is an institution that helps victims of child abuse, and Linda donated her time to record a public service announcement to help raise funds for its charity work. Roy Bechtol was Linda's date at several other social functions that spring, including a party on May 8 to celebrate the filming of the 250th episode of "Dallas."

As Linda Gray's importance on the show has grown, so has her impressive salary. By this point in her blossoming career, she is quickly becoming one of the highest-paid actresses on television. By the time season ten filming began, her salary had soared to $65,000 per episode, with an additional $22,000 for every episode that she directed. It was also revealed that she would now be directing at least *two* episodes per season.

When the tenth season of "Dallas" began to air in the fall of 1987, there were several unanswered questions: Does Pam survive her flaming car crash? (And if so, would another actress portray her?) Would Clayton Farlow suffer a fatal heart attack? And, who would end up with J.R.—Mandy Winger or Sue Ellen?

When Pam Ewing regains consciousness in a Dallas hospital, she finds that she has been disfigured and decides to secretly flee Dallas. In the meantime, several new characters have been introduced into the plot: Bobby's new love interest Lisa Alden (actress Amy Stock), a slick con-man named Casey Denalt (actor

Andrew Stevens), and handsome business consultant Nick Pearce (actor Jack Scalia). Although Sue Ellen's purpose for meeting with Nick Pearce is initially on Valentine Lingerie business, it is clear at their first meeting that romantic sparks are flying.

As the season was being planned, it was announced that Sue Ellen would be pursued by yet another handsome new character on the show. Reportedly, several well-known actors were being considered for the part of Sue Ellen's suitor. Among the celebrities considered for the role were Robert Wagner, Ryan O'Neal, Julio Iglesias, George Hamilton, Kenny Rogers, Roger Moore, Robert Mitchum, and Tony Curtis. From this it would seem that Linda Gray was not exaggerating when she called Sue Ellen the most interesting character on prime-time television!

Several people on the Lorimar staff have discussed the possibility of bringing Victoria Principal back in the role of Pam Ewing in the same way that Bobby Ewing's return was engineered. However, Linda Gray feels that that Principal is firm in her decision to leave the show. "I don't think she would come back," says Linda. "She's too independent."

As long as "Dallas" continues to be a hit show, viewers can rest assured that Linda Gray will be there in front of the cameras as the ever-changeable Sue Ellen Ewing. However, Linda is determined to be involved in show business long after "Dallas" completes its run—whenever that might be. According to her, "I live my life by something my grandmother used to say. My grandmother said, 'I don't want to sit on a porch of an old folks home and ask, 'Why didn't I do that? Why didn't I go to Europe? Or see this movie? Or go to this play? Do it all, and then decide.' I use that philosophy. I try to do it all and then I choose. I feel whatever works for you is magic and you stay there and hone it.

"When I was younger," Linda explains, "I felt like a racehorse at the starting gate—all wound up and excited about life. I wondered when somebody was going to open the gate. Then I realized that I had to open the damn gate myself. And that's what I did. I dragged a little wagon full of shit through life for a long time, and sometimes I've had the hell beat out of me. But my self-awareness and inner strength have kept things in balance, and my curiosity about life keeps me from ever getting too comfortable.

"You know," she proclaims, "I want to live to be a hundred and fifty. There's just so much I want to do, so much I'd like to learn and communicate. I feel brand-new, like a baby. And I'm going for it! I'm just not going to stop having a wonderful time!"

Whether it involves bringing the character of Sue Ellen Ewing to life, directing episodes of hit television shows, appearing in made-for-TV movies, or producing her own projects, Linda Gray has made the commitment to stay active in show business. When she runs out of challenges, she'll simply create new ones for herself. With her self-proclaimed "zest, energy, and enthusiasm for life," Linda is truly television's favorite Renaissance woman—a beautiful "work-in-progress" who is determined not to stop until she has it all!

Linda Gray
Filmography

Palm Springs Weekend (1963; 100 minutes)

Director: Norman Taurog

Cast: Troy Donahue
Connie Stevens
Stephanie Powers
Robert Conrad
Ty Hardin
Jack Weston
Andrew Duggan
Linda Gray

Under the Yum Yum Tree (1963; 110 minutes)

Director: David Swift

Cast: Jack Lemmon
Carol Lynley
Dean Jones
Edie Adams

Imogene Coca
Paul Lynde
Robert Lansing
Linda Gray

Dogs (1976; 90 minutes)
Director: Burt Brinckerhoff
Cast: David McCallum
George Wyner
Eric Server
Sandra McCabe
Sterling Swanson
Linda Gray

Murder in Peyton Place (Made-For-TV, 1977; 100 minutes)
Director: Bruce Kessler
Cast: Christopher Connelly
Dorothy Malone
Ed Nelson
Stella Stevens
Janet Margolin
David Hedison
Tim O'Conner
Linda Gray

The Grass Is Always Greener Over the Septic Tank (Made-For-TV, 1978; 100 minutes)
Director: Robert Day
Cast: Carol Burnett
Charles Grodin
Alex Rocco
Linda Gray
Robert Sampson
Vicki Belmonte
Eric Stoltz

Two Worlds of Jenny Logan (Made-For-TV, 1979; 100 minutes)*

    Director: Frank DiFelitta
        Cast: Lindsay Wagner
                Marc Singer
                Linda Gray
                Alan Feinstein
                Henry Wilcoxon
                Joan Darling
                Constance McCashin

Haywire (Made-For-TV, 1980 200 minutes)

    Director: Michael Tuchner
        Cast: Lee Remick
                Jason Robards
                Deborah Raffin
                Dianne Hull
                Hart Bochner
                Linda Gray
                Dean Jagger
                Richard Johnson

The Wild and the Free (Made-For-TV, 1980; 100 minutes)

    Director: James Hill
        Cast: Linda Gray
                Granville Van Dusen
                Frank Logan
                Ray Forchion
                Sharon Anderson
                Bill Gribble

Not in Front of the Children (Made-For-TV, 1982; 100 minutes)

    Director: Joseph Hardy

---

*available on video cassette

Cast: Linda Gray
John Getz
John Lithgow
Stephen Elliot
Carol Rosen
Cathryn Damon
George Grizzard

The Gambler, Part III—The Legend Continues
(Made-For-TV, 1987; 200 minutes)
Director: Dick Lowry
Cast: Kenny Rogers
Linda Gray
Bruce Boxleitner
Charles Durning
George Kennedy
Jeffrey Jones
Dean Stockwell

Linda Gray
On Television

As a guest star on series:
   "McCloud" (1970s, various episodes)
   "Marcus Welby, M.D." (1970s, various episodes)
   "Switch" (1970s, various episodes)
   "Emergency!" (1970s, various episodes)
   "Big Hawaii" (1977)

As a guest star on specials:
   "Bob Hope in 'The Starmakers'" (1980)
   "Mac Davis—I'll Be Home for Christmas" (1980)
   "The Body Human—The Loving Process" (1981)
   "Night of 100 Stars" (1982)
   "Salute To Lady Liberty" (1984)
   "The Macy's Thanksgiving Day Parade" (1984 and 1986)—Linda Gray and Larry Hagman as host/commentators
   "All-American Thanksgiving Day Parade" (1987)—Linda Gray and Patrick Duffy as host/commentators

146

Linda Gray on Television

As a regular character on series:

"All That Glitters" (1977)
   Character: Linda Murkland

"Dallas" (1978–present)
   Character: Sue Ellen Shepard Ewing
      The five-part mini-series: (April 1978)
      Season One (1978–1979)
      Season Two (1979–1980)
      Season Three (1980–1981)
      Season Four (1981–1982)
      Season Five (1982–1983)
      Season Six (1983–1984)
      Season Seven (1984–1985)
      Season Eight (1985–1986)
      Season Nine (1986–1987)
      Season Ten (1987–1988)

Index

Index

About the Author

Mark Bego is the author of several popular books on the entertainment industry. He has written about television: *TV Rock* (1988), the movies: *The Best of Modern Screen* (St. Martin's Press, 1986) and *Rock Hudson: Public And Private* (1986), and about the lives of many of today's hottest music stars.

Heralded in the press as "the prince of pop music bios," Bego's other books include *Bette Midler: Outrageously Divine* (1987), *Julian Lennon!* (St. Martin's Press, 1986), *Whitney!* (1986), *Sade!* (1986), *Cher!* (1986), *Madonna!* (1985), *On The Road With Michael!* (1984), *The Doobie Brothers* (1980), *The Captain & Tennille* (1977), and *Barry Manilow* (1977). His best-selling Michael Jackson biography, *Michael!* (1984) spent six weeks on *The New York Times* best-seller list, and sold over three million copies in six languages.

For two years Mark was the Editor-In-Chief of *Modern Screen* magazine, and he has appeared frequently on radio and television, talking about the lives and careers of the stars. Mark Bego lives in New York City.